"*I WISH I COULD DRAW*"

HOW TO DO IT

the complete list of titles in the series

THE STUDIO "HOW TO DO IT" SERIES NO. 31
NEW AND REVISED EDITION

"I WISH I COULD DRAW"

by

Percy V. Bradshaw

Principal, The Press Art School

THE STUDIO PUBLICATIONS : LONDON & NEW YORK

First Published 1941
Reprinted 1941
Reprinted 1942
Reprinted 1944
Reprinted 1946
New Edition 1948
Reprinted 1949
Reprinted 1953
Reprinted 1956

(All the illustrations in this book—except those especially attributed to individual artists—were drawn by pupils studying this method of art training, or by members of the author's staff.)

Printed in England by Balding & Mansell Ltd.
Park Works, Wisbech, Cambridgeshire, and published in London by The Studio Ltd., 66 Chandos Place, W.C.2 and in New York by The Studio Publications Inc., 432 Fourth Avenue

CONTENTS

*How Nature teaches line drawing (A pen study
by a pupil who follows Nature's methods)*

FOREWORD

"I *wish* I could draw! But I can't even draw a straight line!"

Are you one of the scores of people whom I've heard making that sadly familiar remark? If so, this little book is going to give you a pleasant surprise. It will prove to you that you *can* draw—that drawing is an absolutely natural form of expression which anybody can use—that it is an inborn instinct which you have merely not developed. This instinct for pictorial expression belongs to all of us; it has demonstrated itself from the earliest days of the world; it has been characteristic of primitive as well as cultured peoples; it has been inseparable from human progress; in fact, it has played an important part in the world's evolution.

Prehistoric man's only method of making a record, or inscribing a message, was by drawing. The writing of today is merely a simplified version of the picture-writing of the past. You proved your pictorial instinct, when you were a youngster, by drawing those matchstick men and women, those quaint animals, those battle-scenes which were mostly smoke, those puffing engines, and other things which broke so much coloured chalk and blunted so many pencils. Later, in your schooldays, your instinct itself was blunted—by Drawing Lessons which converted your natural tendency into a tiresome task.

You were not reminded that Nature, who has provided everything you can want in the wide world, was waiting to provide you with ideal lessons. You were not told that Nature demonstrates—in every single plant, flower, or living organism—a complete system of Art theory and practice. Doesn't it comfort you to know that it isn't too late to learn—that Nature imposes no age-limit on her pupils? She is waiting to teach you, NOW!

You have merely to join her class, and watch her at work. Every stage of her tuition is completely worked out; you can progress, as she does, from small beginnings to big developments—from seed to fruit; she dictates the obvious steps to be taken, and provides you with innumerable examples. And, given the opportunity, she will soon make it plain that all we understand by "Art" is not just a special gift for a few, but a part of life itself; simple, easily understood, and opening the way to happiness of the spirit.

In my capacity as Principal of The Press Art School, I have employed Nature's principles of teaching with conspicuous success for over 35 years, and have trained thousands of students, many of whom now bear well-known names. If you will apply these methods systematically and conscientiously, I can promise that you, too, will not be disappointed.

Eight printings have been called for since this book was first published in 1941, and I wish to express my gratitude to innumerable readers who have acknowledged the pleasure they have derived from this introduction to drawing. I have been able to incorporate additional instructions and many new illustrations in this edition, which may, I hope, provide you with the key to Nature's own system of Art training.

PERCY V. BRADSHAW.

HOW NATURE TEACHES
LINE DRAWING

THE LINES in a leaf, if we know how to read them, convey as exact and definite an idea as do letters in handwriting; and for that reason, if we wish to express anything—especially if we wish to represent Nature's work—we must study lines from their source to their end.

It is possible for lines in a good drawing to convey almost anything within the knowledge of man, and your work will indicate, whether you like it or not, either weakness, insipidity, disorder or order, strength, understanding or beauty—according as you learn the value and use of line.

Line work offers, in a few splendid touches, the ability to declare to the beholder what it might take pages of words to do, and what words could not do even then; and it may do instantly what a symphony of music might fail to explain. This is your power—if you think first, observe with the eye, and then draw.

It will enable you to write down in pictures what you think, read, do, or see, and it is an accomplishment that everyone should possess as they possess handwriting.

To be a fine artist in line, you must start systematically observing, comparing and analysing.

Watch Nature in winter, in bare masts; note the amazing variety of lines shown by bushes, shrubs, hedges, trees, when seen clear against the sky; compare the radiating bare lines of a naked tree with the same tree clothed with leaves.

Notice the completely different shapes of various types of leaf, and the corresponding shapes of the outline of the tree, and realise how trees sometimes agree in general shape with the outline of their leaves.

A garden, a park, a tree-lined road or a country lane can be a perpetual joy to you at all seasons if you use your eyes and develop your pictorial observation. And the study of the more obvious lines which such Nature-objects provide is a splendid practice for the more subtle study of human and animal types, which we will consider soon.

The *studies* for this first lesson in art principally relate to the value of the Point and the Line.

Before commencing actual work you will require some drawing materials. Fortunately these are of the simplest character. For line drawing you need some good pencils—of grades HB and B—some drawing pens, good smooth firm white drawing paper, a bottle of Indian ink, piece of rubber, drawing pins, and a board on which to support your paper.

The drawing board can be a piece of 4 or 5 plywood about 20 × 15 inches. It is possible to buy a more substantial board at an artist's colourman, but the simpler board is entirely adequate at this stage, and much cheaper.

You can even dispense with the drawing board if you work on a sketch-block or stoutly-bound sketchbook.

The acorn and the oak are fit introductions to Nature's methods. There is very little about the drawings which calls for comment. They are simply diagrams, but there is something rather worth your attention in the confident quality of line in the sprig of leaves and acorns.

In the three little diagrams, a, b and c, we see Art adopting Nature's principle, starting with the point, first defining the centre of the object, and then working towards the circumference, perfectly indicating the boundary marks of the object.

In the diagram b we observe line work starting, a single line having grown to "enclosed" or "enclosing lines."

In the diagram c, Art's representation of a solid is shown in a very simple form.

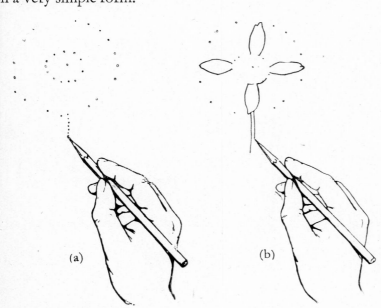

(a)   (b)   (c)

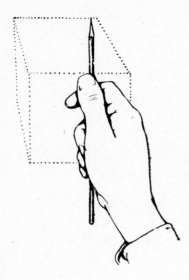

Figure 2 shows a simple method of measurement. Try this—the pencil being held in a perpendicular or upright position, at arm's length, between your eye and the object you are drawing. Close one eye and check off, with your thumb, that portion of the pencil's length which covers any main proportion of your object. Then compare this proportion to any other relative measurement which will enable you to gauge roughly the proportionate sizes—for example, the length of a figure with its breadth, the length of the arms in relation to the legs.

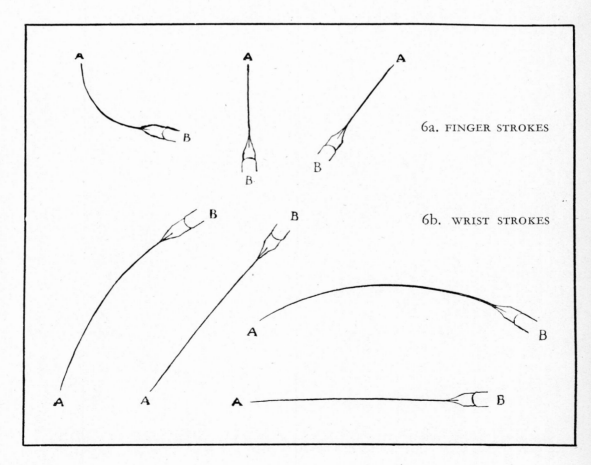

6a. FINGER STROKES

6b. WRIST STROKES

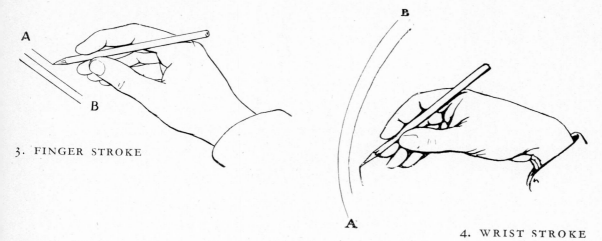

3. FINGER STROKE

4. WRIST STROKE

Figure 3 shows you a method of holding the pencil or pen in drawing. This method is exactly similar to that normally used in writing.

Figure 4 represents a wrist stroke, useful in making pliable, sweeping, graceful lines or curves. The wrist is used freely here, the pencil or pen point being *towards* you at the commencement of the line, and the direction of the stroke being away from the body, as the letters A and B indicate.

Figure 5 is a suggestion of a full arm stroke made with charcoal or pencil, a straight line being drawn downwards, at arm's length, with the drawing-surface almost perpendicular, or at the ordinary slope provided by a drawing-board resting on an easel.

5. FULL ARM STROKE

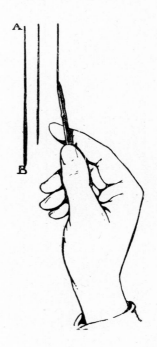

Figure 6 on the opposite page, gives further examples of pen strokes, but for purposes of simplification, I have omitted the diagrams of the hand. I feel, however, that these simple little illustrations will be perfectly clear.

The three finger-strokes give examples of lines made by the method shown in figure 3—that is, with the pen used almost exactly as it is in writing, the direction of the lines being from A to B in each case.

The four diagrams which follow all show wrist strokes, the wrist being used in a pliable manner, as indicated by figure 4. This stroke encourages pliability of line, and gives delightful command over the pen, when you have had a certain amount of practice. If you try these exercises in pencils and pens of all kinds, you will soon become familiar with your materials.

Each medium has its special uses and its particular touch

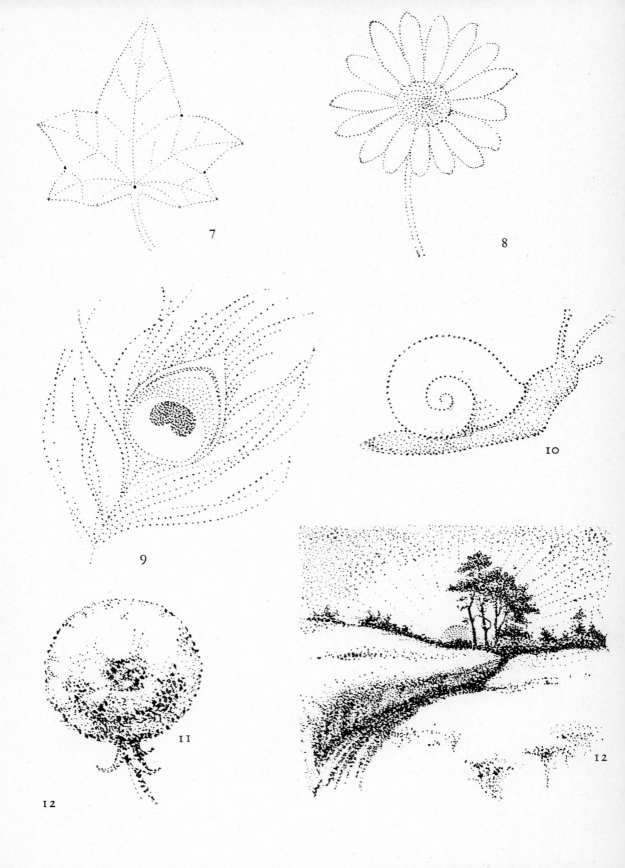

and value. Charcoal, for instance, is valuable because it produces great masses and depths of tone, with the least possible effort, and as it is easily rubbed or dusted out, it is used frequently in sketching out a subject.

The dot, point, or centre, is used with two objects: firstly, to show its value in finding the centre and principle landmarks of a drawing; secondly, to indicate its fascinating quality in pen and ink technique.

When you make your point studies I want you to show the same care, subtlety and cleanliness of treatment as you find in our examples on the opposite page.

In the Ivy leaf study you will see the chief points to be considered in starting your first point drawing. After fixing the main points, north, south, east and west, with pencil marks, you should form the outline lightly with pencil. Then mark the positions of important features within that outline; such as the shapes of the daisy petals, and the "eye" of the feather. You will then continue the construction in pencil *lines*, and complete the point-work with a pen.

There is one detail I should like particularly to emphasize in figures 7, 8, 9, 10. They have a definite, precise character in the pen touch. Every dot has a certain careful shape, it is placed sincerely on the paper, and the pupil has not relied on dots *in a mass* to create his effect. I want you, from the outset of your work, to be equally careful with every touch you put on your paper. Avoid carelessness. Determine that every touch of your pencil or pen shall beautify your drawing surface—*not* disfigure it.

In figures 11 and 12, the pupil has resorted somewhat to splashes instead of clean, well-shaped dots. This is particularly the case in the puffball, which is shaded more or less with a series of blots instead of dots.

In the little landscape there is a certain attraction, and you may be tempted to try your hand at something equally ambitious, but I very strongly advise you not to. You are to regard this illustration as a diagram only—a mere hint to you as to the decorative possibilities of the point.

I don't want you to try ambitious types of work for this lesson. You will have an opportunity of doing so at later stages. And *don't* copy the illustrations. Copying is lazy and unnecessary, now that you have a chance to do original work direct from natural or other objects.

FIRST EXERCISES

IN POINT DRAWING

13

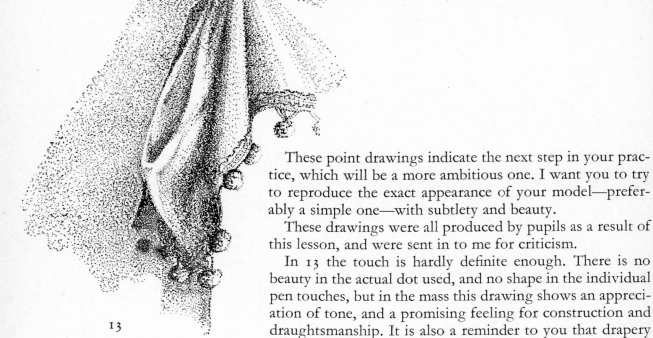

13

These point drawings indicate the next step in your practice, which will be a more ambitious one. I want you to try to reproduce the exact appearance of your model—preferably a simple one—with subtlety and beauty.

These drawings were all produced by pupils as a result of this lesson, and were sent in to me for criticism.

In 13 the touch is hardly definite enough. There is no beauty in the actual dot used, and no shape in the individual pen touches, but in the mass this drawing shows an appreciation of tone, and a promising feeling for construction and draughtsmanship. It is also a reminder to you that drapery is a useful subject for point work, when other objects may not be available.

14 is a much better specimen technically, and, as a first lesson study it is particularly creditable. It has required a great deal of observation and sincerity to suggest the surface-markings as well as they are indicated here. The cast shadow shows a

The point-drawings on these two pages were first-lesson studies by my pupils.

14

15

14

tendency to run into a blot in one portion; but, altogether, this drawing is far above the average of a first-lesson point study, and is well worth consideration as a specimen of technique.

15 is well constructed, but the shadow thrown from the object is a little bit too obtrusive and heavy. Obviously the nearer detail of the shell itself should be bolder than the treatment of the shadow. You must remember that distant details ought to be introduced with more delicate dots than those in the foreground. In fact there should be progressive and gradual increase in the size of your dots from background to foreground.

16 shows more "spaciousness" and more purity of technique. The dots are well shaped, definite and confident. They are not quite so crowded as they are in the other specimens, and, in a broad, easy and very effective way, the student has appreciated not only the constructional peculiarities of the object, but its actual texture and surface. Because it is so cleanly, openly and definitely drawn, it is a very useful object lesson in treatment.

The last studies of the boot and the glove are among the very best point drawings produced by any student. In the first place, the draughtsmanship is sincere; then there has been the most thorough appreciation of texture and light and shade: finally, the dots themselves are admirable in shape.

When, by practical experiment, you have realised the value of the point—both as a factor in elementary construction, and a method of technique, known to professional artists as stipple—you will be able to proceed with greater confidence to the study of *line*.

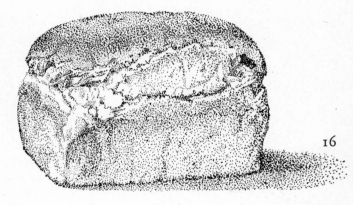

16

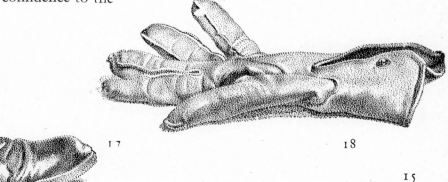

17

18

15

VALUE OF THE LINE

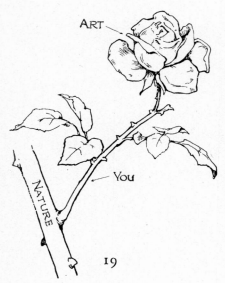

We commence with a simple pictorial symbol, "Nature, you and Art," which will be a reminder to you of the principles on which these lessons are based.

The second diagram, "Mind and Eye" is introduced as another illustration of the necessity for proper observation —seeing the object and getting it impressed on your brain before you begin to draw.

Take a flower—the simplest you can find—say a field or ox-eye daisy. How is one to begin?

Follow Nature's plan; let the flower "begin itself"—in your mind. Take it into your mind exactly as it is before you, observe it and *think* about it; in other words, let Nature begin the work. "Well begun is half done." Familiarity takes away half the fear.

Before commencing serious drawing, observe the general facts:—1. It's there—a flower—it has life. 2. It has colour. 3. It has form.

These are the facts you notice, and they follow each other as you have observed them. But form is of more importance to you just now than colour, for you are about to represent only that form on your paper.

From this simple start you may proceed to measurements, each of which can first be indicated with a point or dot, until you have a ground plan, or skeleton indication, of the form of your flower. It will only be a mere map—a flat, second-

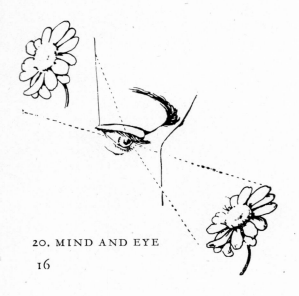

20. MIND AND EYE

21. LOOK AT THE OBJECT

dimensional thing, without life—a series of measurements; but from this start you can proceed to show the *vitality* of that living flower in front of you.

In the previous pages you have been shown that you must begin to draw by an orderly plan. First find the centre of your flower, and indicate it by a dot on your paper. Then judge and indicate the circumference of the flower by four other points—one at the top, one at the bottom, one on the left, and one at the right, so that you have a preliminary indication of the height and width of your flower—points of the compass, north, south, east and west.

At this stage, you will begin to use three main types of elementary line, which will form the basis of all your drawing. Let us realise their significance and possibilities.

You will observe that I divide lines into three types—straight, curved and bent. These again are sub-divided, but figure 23 on the next page will remind you how Nature uses lines of these types.

The *straight* line is one which expresses supporting power, as in stems, grasses, etc. The *curved* line is used in myriads of ways, for the outlines of leaves, flowers, etc.; but it is useful to consider it as a containing or holding line. You will see that so many of Nature's curves are used for this purpose, and we illustrate the simple little cup of the acorn as an instance.

The *bent* or changing line is also used in an infinity of ways —in branches, stems, twigs, grasses, etc.

22. EXAMPLE OF BAD WORK
WEAK AND SCRATCHY LINE

CONSTRUCTIONAL DETAILS

STUDY THE COLOUR

ELEMENTARY LINES USED

B

17

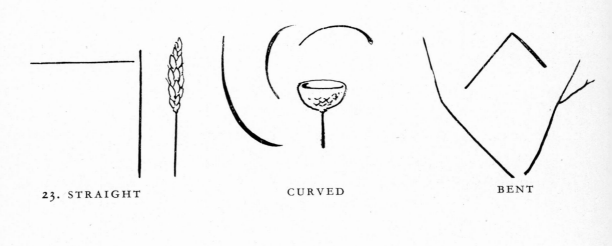

23. STRAIGHT · CURVED · BENT

24. THICKNESS AND
THINNESS OF LINE

25 and **26.** HOW THREE LINES COMBINE TO GIVE
MOVEMENT AND CHARACTER

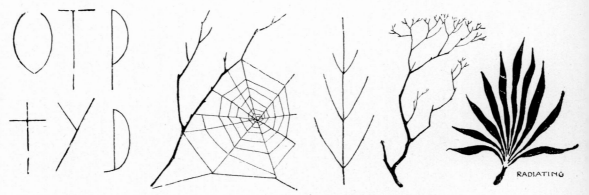

27. HOW LINES JOIN, GROW AND RADIATE

Now, I want you to remember these types of line—the *straight*, the *curved* and the *bent*—as they will help you to reduce very difficult and complicated natural objects to their simplest essentials.

Figure 24 shows you that variety in the thickness or thinness of straight and curved lines has its importance, and you won't do many drawings before you appreciate that the increase in the thickness of a line here and there has a remarkable value.

In 25 you are shown simple combinations of two or three pliable lines. 26 shows the three lines in rather more comprehensive form. First there is the straight line, which expresses a certain weight and solidity. Then there is the bent or forked line, suggesting rapid movement. Thirdly, there is a graceful, long, sweeping line, which might indicate the roll of a wave, or any other undulating surface. The other diagrams are elementary indications of curved and angular lines, used for various purposes, suggestions of height and depth, covering or holding.

27 is an indication of the straight, curved and bent lines used in lettering and conventional decorative shapes, while the cobweb and accompanying diagrams give a slightly more pictorial idea as to how lines join, grow and radiate in Nature.

The final figure, 28, is another proof of how effectively well-shaped lines, even of a simple character, can represent the most complicated and elaborate subjects.

28. HOW NATURE'S THREE ELEMENTS ARE REPRESENTED IN LINE

The artist, then, has three chief forms of line with which to interpret Nature. He must learn to use the three in one, if he would produce Nature's round effect and meaning.

Again we commence with a diagram which shows how Nature develops in line from the seed to the root and stem, as discussed earlier.

Secondly, you are given some examples of lines used in Nature and Art, to convey the effect of life. The figure of the seated man and the duck show important preliminary lines which suggest the character of the object, and you will realise a little later, with what advantage the principle of observing "Life Lines" in an object, helps you in drawing.

In figure 32, you are shown how the facility you have acquired in handwriting can be of value in drawing, and how the ordinary, simple curves in the drawing of a leaf should not present very much greater difficulty for you than those curves which you form so easily in the shaping of your letters. Try this experiment yourself. It will be an interesting form of manual exercise. Commence by drawing the penstrokes used in forming the single letter J. Then gradually increase the size of your letters, until the capitals are three or four inches high.

When you discover, as you soon will do, that you can draw large, sweeping, graceful curves, try variations of other letters in handwriting—all the letters with loops and graceful down strokes, such as A, B, F, G, H, I, etc.

You can, with advantage, experiment in this way with almost every letter of the alphabet, as these exercises will help you greatly to acquire ease in handling the pen. There is no particular artistic or inspirational value to be gained by such an exercise, but it will develop your manual dexterity considerably.

In figures 33 and 34 you get illustrations of natural lines and curves. In the first you are shown simple ways in which Nature introduces variations of straight, curved and angular lines, while the curves are also pleasant developments of more graceful pen strokes.

29

30

31

32. CURVES IN HANDWRITING AND NATURE   33. NATURAL LINES

34. NATURAL CURVES

35. JOINING AND GROWING LINES

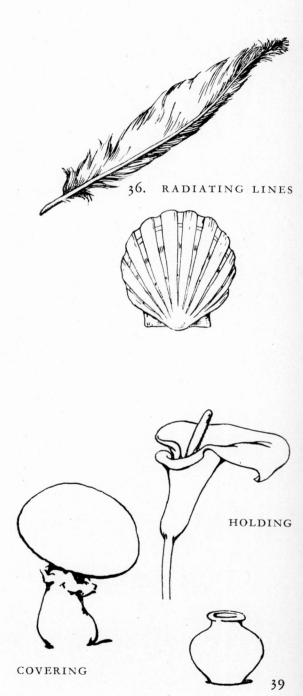

36. RADIATING LINES

37. STRAIGHT AND BENT LINES
SUPPORTING AND BRANCHING

HOLDING

38

COVERING

39

Here are some more simple but important types of line to be found in Nature. In the first diagram, you see some joining or growing lines. The feather and shell are simple examples of lines which radiate, while below are some diagrams showing those which are straight, bent, supporting and branching, with some covering or holding lines.

You will get evidence of the value of a well-chosen line in figures 38 and 40. The little bird is put in with Japanese directness and simplicity; in the puppy the actual texture of the coat is most vigorously suggested by the fat, crisp, alert, bristling pen strokes.

Effects of this kind are not produced by carelessness, and it is only because there is not a single careless touch here, that the artist has got so much value out of his lines.

I hope you are beginning to understand why I insist so strongly on the necessity for every one of your lines being put down with care from your very earliest efforts. You must *begin right*.

In handwriting, you had first to learn to use two or three simple forms thoroughly and carefully. "Handwriting" is of the same vital importance in drawing, and success is only to be achieved with the same method—by beginning right.

The curved line stands for movement—holding or joining —continuation. You need to know how to use the curve so as not to destroy the value of continuation of your straight line.

A crooked or bent line is the outcome of one line from another, and it must develop in unity with the original purpose of the line from which it proceeds.

Keep in your mind, always, the idea of *growth*. You cannot find a single line in Nature unsupported by something. Your lines will grow more easily and beautifully if you let them grow from each other with a healthy purpose, and with the spring of life.

You will soon see that strength and life is given by the proper *joining* of a line—that weakness and want of life comes from weak drawing. Your lines *must not* trail off indefinitely just where they should swing strongly into one another.

40

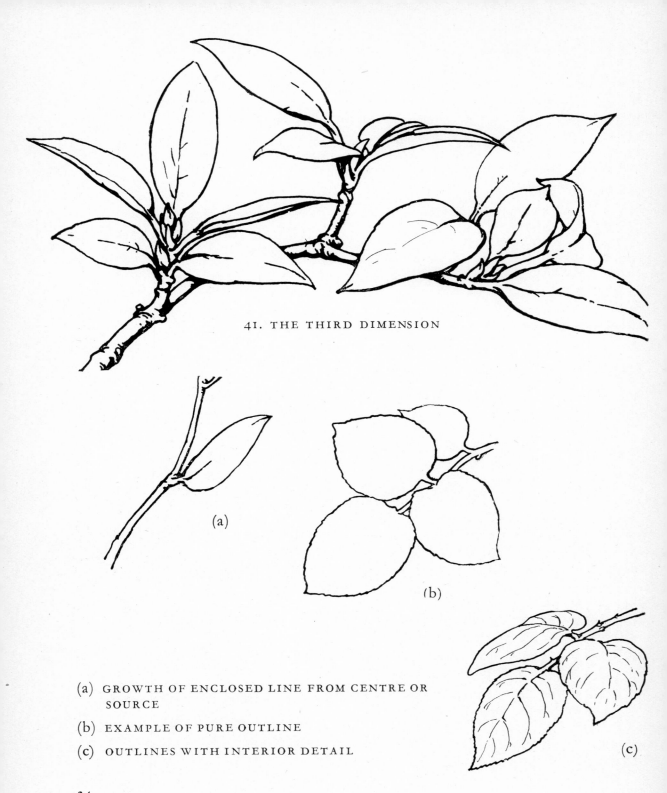

41. THE THIRD DIMENSION

(a)

(b)

(a) GROWTH OF ENCLOSED LINE FROM CENTRE OR
    SOURCE

(b) EXAMPLE OF PURE OUTLINE

(c) OUTLINES WITH INTERIOR DETAIL

(c)

A drawing in the *first dimension* consists of one "measurement" *only*—that of length *or* height—without breadth or thickness. This dimension is best expressed or represented by a single line.

A drawing in the *second dimension* contains two of the measurements together, length *and* breadth, and these are expressed most generally by designs, shapes, or decorative patterns, drawn flatly—without light and shade.

A drawing in the *third dimension* completely represents the three measurements together—length, breadth *and* thickness. To suggest depth or thickness in a drawing adequately, necessitates careful realisation and representation of light and shade.

Figure 41, forms an excellent example of what can be done with clean, vigorous, bold line, and touches of solid black to suggest the third dimension.

To simplify our study of the three dimensions, we should regard a single stem as Nature's equivalent of the first dimension, a flat leaf as a second dimensional object, and fruit or flowers as objects containing the three dimensions.

In reality, even the thinnest stem is a third dimensional object, containing, as it does, length, breadth and thickness. We therefore, ask you to regard the stem, leaf and fruit as *symbols* only—for the better and simpler explanation of our theory.

The second diagram (b), in figure 41, an example in pure outline, as it makes no attempt to suggest the thickness of the object, is a second-dimensional study, while the third of the diagrams (c) "outlines with interior detail" is third-dimensional, the suggestion of interior detail and one or two clever little touches of black having made all the difference between a flat pattern and a simple study of the third dimension.

Figure 42 illustrates Nature's equivalent to the elementary types of shape—circle, oval (or pointed ellipse) and the angular types, represented by the triangle and square.

ENCLOSING LINES, OR THE SECOND DIMENSION

42.
EXAMPLES OF ELEMENTARY SHAPES IN NATURE

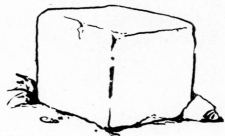

THE THIRD DIMENSION

A DRAWING in the *third dimension*—as I have already stated —completely represents the three measurements of length, breadth and thickness. This necessitates an understanding of light and shade in its simpler, broader aspects.

In subsequent lessons it will be taken for granted that you have a thorough grasp of the requirements of simple line technique, and that is why it is so necessary, in these earlier instructions, to reiterate simple facts as to the value of each individual line you can use.

Before attempting to develop our use of line one stage further, in the complete representation of the solid, let us see exactly what we are aiming at in the final result. We will discuss the means to that end afterwards, and then, as before, set you to work on practical experiments.

You have already considered the partial representation of the solid, by means of an outline of varied thickness, assisted by a representation of the essential surface markings. The next step is to combine, with these, the lines of shading which are to complete the illusion of three-dimensional form.

43. *The drawings of the apple are examples of clean elementary line studies in which solidity, light and shade, and texture are all considered.*

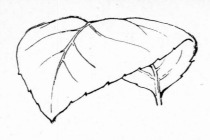
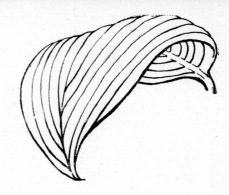

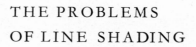

When you have a good idea of the broad range of tones on the surface you are about to shade, your next consideration must be for the *direction, character* and *quality* of the lines you are to use in representing these tones. You have already explored some of their possibilities in the previous lesson. It will be helpful now if we consider the case of the apple, figure 43, as an example of one problem of light and shade.

In deciding upon the *direction* of line in shading, our accumulated knowledge of the character of an apple helps our observation. Its smooth roundness of form, and its growth around the core in the centre, naturally suggest that the shading lines should follow the contours of surface from one end of the core to the other. The "quarters" of a peeled orange give you an exact plan of the general line-direction in the shading of these round fruits—or, at least, a plan it is wisest to follow in your first experiments. And, in whatever position you place your apple, the shading lines should pass smoothly round its surface and flow into the upper and lower parts of the outline as though they were actually passing to the rear where the eye cannot reach.

THE PROBLEMS OF LINE SHADING

44. *These leaf studies will remind you of the stages through which you have passed.*

The pupils' drawings on these two pages give further illustrations of the value of expressive line. There is nothing very ambitious about either the brush, the fan or the thick tassels, but in all these drawings, the pupils have realised that each article required its characteristic touch.

The half-dozen drawings are particularly good in their feeling for the right touch. The coal was perhaps the most difficult of the six, and it is notable for the strength and vigour with which the nearer details are introduced. It illustrates, once again, a principle which has to be observed in all good pen work—that nearer details should be represented by stronger lines than those which are further away.

Notice the direction from which light falls upon the object before you, and how, in striking the surface, it drives away the shadows to the remoter side.

In commencing shading, you must study, first of all, those gradations of tone and colour which lie within the outline, and which bind the constructional details and outline together into a perfect whole. These are the questions you should ask yourself:

What *is* the texture? Smooth or rough, delicate or coarse, broken or rugged, silky or furry, dull or shiny?

What *length* of line would best indicate its precise qualities? Should the lines be long, graceful and pliable—mechanically unvaried—short and spasmodic—flowing—thick, or thin?

What *directions* should the lines take?

You have three definite means of achieving that line variety which constitutes so much of the charm of a pen drawing. You have to consider character, direction and spacing.

By varying your line quality in these three ways, you can, as we shall see, represent almost any texture or surface.

EXERCISES

IN LIGHT

SHADE AND

TEXTURE

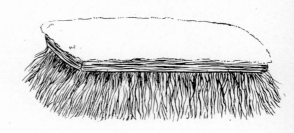

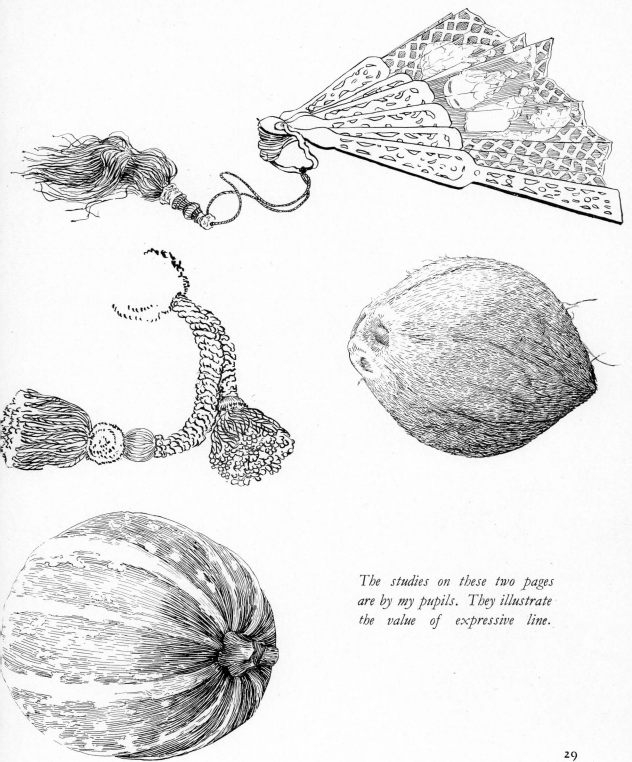

The studies on these two pages
are by my pupils. They illustrate
the value of expressive line.

29

Look, then, particularly for the edges of your objects, and further, for the edges of the characteristic interior masses. When you begin to study trees, masses of foliage, etc., you will be shown how this analysis of complicated masses can give you attractive simplification, and how a careful treatment of the edges solves such a large part of your problems.

The drawings below call for very little comment. The difference in texture between the gorse and the rocks on the left is quite evidently considered thoroughly. The short, feathery types of pen stroke in the interior shading of the drake also has its value, though the outline is, frankly, monotonous and rather unsympathetic.

The pages you have just studied should impress you thoroughly with the extraordinary possibilities of intelligent line work in the suggestion of almost every variety of texture and I hope you will apply all this knowledge in your work.

A respect for every line you put down is exceedingly important at this stage. It is a discipline which will affect all your future work, and if by chance you are wondering how this feeling for line variety is going to influence the more ambitious drawings you will attempt in the future, you will soon be able to provide your own evidence.

HOW
CAREFUL SHAPING
OF LINE
FORMS TEXTURE

LANDSCAPE

You will, I think, realise why I have commenced the illustration of this lesson with a few pictorial reminders of the value of line.

Line has been your principal medium up to now, and it will remain, for some time to come, your chief method of expression. It is vitally important, in attempting to draw landscape or landscape details in pen-and-ink, that you should keep in view the necessity for putting down each single line with careful consideration for its responsibilities. Even when you are suggesting broad areas of tone, individual lines are important; where you are representing intricate details, and the variety of textures which are to be seen in every landscape, character of line is most important.

Let us remind ourselves once again, then, of the principal line-characteristics which have been observed from the commencement of the lessons—the straight, curved, and bent line; the necessity for analysing growth and appreciating the difference of touch and texture in various objects; pliability of line, etc. You have already seen several proofs of the success with which a mere pen point, rightly controlled, can suggest the effects of light and shade, and the characteristics of even subtle textures and surfaces.

Only by considering Nature as a friend, and studying natural objects with affection, can you represent them with sympathy and understanding. You must never regard a Nature subject as a tiresome exercise. If you do, there is something completely wrong about your outlook, and the lessons of this method have been wasted on you.

I want you to realise that the correct representation of even the simplest Natural object needs thought and care, that a certain beauty and purity of line is imperative, and that the

SIMPLE DIAGRAMS OF CHARACTERISTIC GROWTHS

careful shaping of every one of your lines is just as necessary in making (or "growing") a good drawing, as the growth of a perfect natural object is dependent on the health and vigour of its various stages.

Simple and effective though these apparently casual sketches are, they give evidence of a lot of observation, and you will only succeed in your work by using sincerity and thought in every one of your sketches and studies.

Continuing our consideration of line, you will find on these pages several valuable suggestions and reminders as to what to look for in drawing trees and suggesting varied natural surfaces.

Edges are vitally important in tree-study, and, in observing a mass of foliage, you should adopt the method of analysing the foliage first through half-closed eyes, selecting the principal masses, and then searching for the particular character of outline indicated by the tree itself and by its interior portions.

You will see, in the opposite group of diagrams, what I mean. These are by no means detailed drawings, nor are they as sincere as they should be. They are merely sketchy indications of what to look for; but, even in their incomplete state, they do, I am sure, indicate how much variety can be imparted to a drawing, and how important it is that the characteristic edges and textures should be observed and represented thoroughly.

Each tree has its special characteristics of shape, growth and texture, and it is a most fascinating study to endeavour to represent the chief characteristics in line.

I hope that these little sketches—which, once again, I would remind you are to be considered merely as explanatory *diagrams*—will inspire you to produce something much more ambitious.

Don't hurry. Speed will come later. I would only ask, at this stage for thoroughly careful observation and drawing, no matter how long this takes.

A FEW "DON'TS"

Don't tackle studies in the wrong order. The order followed in these pages illustrates the sequence of thought in the lessons, and will simplify your problems.

Don't start the pen work without complete pencil preparation. The point, as well as the line studies, must be drawn carefully in pencil first. Shape or construct your objects accurately before "finishing" with pen-and-ink.

BEECHES IN HURSLEY PARK

A PUPIL'S DRAWING IN TWO STAGES

The careful study of the character of trees, and sincere practice in drawing them, can produce most gratifying results, as many of my pupils have discovered. This tree study, shown in two stages, should be of considerable encouragement and assistance to you. Observe first of all, how crisply and cleanly your fellow-pupil has drawn the trees, and how effectively he has analysed and represented what must have been a very subtle and confusing effect of light and shade. The drawing is as sunny as it is simple and sincere; and the preliminary pencil shading has been very useful as an aid to deciding on the best direction for pen lines.

The conversion of the pencil drawing into pen and ink has necessarily been a little disappointing. One can never, in pen and ink, obtain the subtle softness of effect which is possible in pencil, and it needs a very clever pen

draughtsman indeed to vary his line quality sufficiently to suggest approximately the contrasts of colour. Once again, all the drawing and construction of this subject has been carried through conscientiously; the direction of line is very suitable throughout, as it follows logically the forms and contours of the surfaces. But the big tree in the foreground needs more strength and variety of line. The nearer branches should be introduced with gradually stronger and bolder lines; instead of which, the nearest branch is rather tighter and closer in line than the shading of the upper part of the main trunk. Further, there are worrying spots of black introduced into the tree trunk on the left. But I have no doubt you will be quite satisfied if, in your early studies of trees from Nature, you achieve as successful a drawing as this pupil has produced. You will soon discover that you are involved in problems of light and shade, as well as of construction. Let us, then, give some thought to elementary aspects of this subject as it affects landscape.

THE LIGHTING ASPECT

This series of sketches indicates the immense variety of the lighting aspect. These simple drawings, if studied in conjunction with Nature, will do much to help you to observe how infinitely varied are the different effects which are constantly passing before us. Light from all angles, reflections, and their manifold subtleties—all these are to be studied and analysed with the greatest care.

Observe the *direction* of light; then, having resolved which particular effect you desire to depict, resolutely stick to it, and do not be disturbed by the fact that the effect changes. Wait for the chosen effect to reappear, as it usually will, several times within the hour.

You must make absolutely certain of the lightest and darkest tones of the planes and masses. Pick out the lightest spot and the darkest spot, knowing that nothing can be lighter than the lightest, and nothing can be darker than the

a

a. LIGHT FROM RIGHT

b. LIGHT OVERHEAD

c. LIGHT IN FRONT

darkest. All other tones or values come between these, and each should be related to and compared with these two important spots.

In landscape work the relative "values" are of the utmost importance. "Values" is a term used to indicate the relative difference in the value of one light or dark as compared with the remaining lights or darks. The term also extends to colour, "colour values" being the relative warmths or coolnesses of the parts of the object in light as well as in shade. For instance, a whitewashed wall with a yellow spot on it would have the light flowing equally all over it, and all parts would be equal in *light* value, but not equal in colour value.

The darks in Nature "lose off"—or lose strength—sooner than the lights, as they both become more enveloped in atmosphere.

b

c

SKETCH, STUDY, AND PICTURE

The landscape painter or draughtsman is an object of sincere compassion—almost of contemptuous interest—to the hardy individual who tills the soil, and whose only thought is whether it will be fine or stormy, if it is "good growing weather," and so on.

To a timber merchant, a tree represents so much wood, and rarely anything more. Except to an artist, the sky is seldom or ever looked at from the point of view of admiration or wonder; others regard the heavens as the place where one can get an indication as to whether it is necessary to carry an umbrella or not.

But let us come to the real consideration of what the word landscape means to the artist.

Your landscape work that is done from Nature, divides itself into three stages, the *sketch*, the *study*, the *picture*.

A sketch aims frankly at expressing the emotion felt by the artist at some particular effect or scene. It must be absolutely spontaneous. And even though it be but a few blots, notes, scratches on paper, smudges of charcoal, etc., if it conveys that particular effect—for example, the hurried movement of a sky, an effect of travelling light or shade—the object of making the sketch has been achieved. But the "blots," etc., be it understood, must always have definite intention and purpose. A good sketch is *not* a collection of meaningless lines; it should convey, vigorously and correctly, the impressions aimed at.

Opposite is a sketch, approached from the point of view of relative tone values, simply expressed. It suggests the type of sketch your present experiments are leading to. Here the medium is soft pencil, tone being added to the previously drawn outline.

Now, we can consider two sketches by an artist who relies on line, and who is famous as a specialist in architecture—Sydney R. Jones—who has achieved a world-wide reputation.

The certainty of his approach, and the precision of his line are obvious in these sketches. Note the variety of treatment in his quick impression of the Wye Valley—the light but firm touch with which he has analysed the background hills, the concentration of tone on the middle distance, and the stronger line with which he has emphasised the foreground. There is no fumbling or hesitation here! He is equally decisive in the sketch on the next page—a rapid note at Arnhem, in which the characteristic architectural details are recorded with such satisfying sureness.

SYDNEY R. JONES: THE WYE VALLEY

SYDNEY R. JONES: ARNHEM-ON-RHINE

I call your special attention to the sketch below and those on the two following pages. They are by that distinguished landscape painter, Bertram Nicholls, P.R.B.A., who has kindly allowed me to use them. He especially asked me, however, to emphasize that they were merely painter's sketches—not examples of the art of pencil drawing, but "raw material" and information of the kind on which he has based his pictures. He had no idea, when he made them, that you, or anyone else, would see this work, which was as private as notes in his diary—but I am grateful to him for allowing us to study them.

Look at the sunshine he has suggested in this very free

BERTRAM NICHOLLS, P.R.B.A.

pencil drawing—the decisive analysis of the shapes of the tree-masses, the touches of shading which so effectively emphasize them, and the valuable contrast he has given to them by the stronger tone of the foreground banks and the overhanging foliage. This is a painter's "note," a rapid impression in which he had no time to consider quality of pencil technique. It was made—as are most of his sketches—on a sheet of smoothish paper, 15 inches by 11, with a 6B pencil.

He regards the lighting aspect as immensely important, reminding us that a subject which has little pictorial interest at one hour of the day, may be magnificent at another.

He advises beginners approaching landscape to indicate the main lines of their subject very lightly, until they are reasonably sure that all the planes of foreground, middle distance and distance are in right relationship.

On these pages he has recorded architecture, and you will observe how decisively he has drawn the constructional details, first indicating them with confident, decisive outlines and then registering the chief masses of tone. Below the study of the castle is the first rough note, in which he tried out the possibilities of the subject as a composition. If the principal interest is architecture, he will draw that most definitely, merely hinting at the foliage —or vice versa. But he keeps the entire subject in his mind all the time, for it is the composition as a whole that he wishes to capture as subsequent material for his pictures, which, though influenced by the fine English tradition of Richard Wilson, Cotman, Cozens and Reynolds, are alight with his own distinction.

BERTRAM
NICHOLLS
P.R.B.A.

BERTRAM
NICHOLLS, P.R.B.A.

43

We continue our study of architectural drawing with a pen sketch by Sydney Jones, and follow with three examples of pencil drawings by that very popular and versatile artist Fred Taylor, R.I.

The pen drawing of the old lych-gate below will remind you of the realism which can be achieved by accurate drawing of architectural detail, even when the main essentials are recorded in little more than outline, with a few indications of texture. Here, Sydney Jones was simply concerned with construction; the economy of line and the precision of every touch will, I hope, influence your own work with the pen.

The pencil drawings by Fred Taylor which follow, will be a further object-lesson; they are examples of the work he enjoys as a relief from painting pictures for the R.A., R.I., and other exhibitions, designing posters, illustrating travel books, and other work in which he excels. He talks with a schoolboy's enthusiasm of his "holidays with a pencil" when he has been able to wander around sketching "just for the joy of it."

You will observe the apparently loose freedom of his line and the remarkable suggestion of colour he achieves by the emphasis of his darks. He uses a soft pencil—a 6B if possible —not only on account of the variety of tone it can provide, but because the use of a soft lead imposes its own discipline. You have to put down each touch very carefully with a 6B, unless you want to produce smeary masses. He is never happier than during these carefree days when he has his "studio in his pocket"—simply a supply of paper and a few pencils, and can do exactly as he likes.

In starting a sketch he uses the pencil a great deal for "eye-measurement," to test the relative heights and widths of the buildings he is drawing. He begins by fixing the nearest vertical line, then measures the position of the next

SYDNEY R. JONES

FRED TAYLOR, R.I.

vertical, putting them down on the paper lightly, but carefully, afterwards establishing the other main constructional proportions of windows, doorways, roofs, etc. When all these main facts are established, in outline, he "goes for" the shapes of the main *shadows*, which give solidity and stability to his work.

He only puts down on paper what he regards as absolutely necessary, and tries to keep his shadows luminous. He warns you against overloading a pencil sketch with broad areas of tone, and sticks to his conviction that "the paper has to do most of the work." Throughout, his touch is sensitive; you will see how remarkably he manages to suggest colour and atmosphere by the delicate precision of his outlines and the placing of his darks. But please realise that the *exact* shapes of these fascinating little darks in windows and doorways, roofs and cornices, must be recorded.

If you study his work carefully you cannot fail to notice the remarkable effects he obtains by his very accurate, sensitive drawing of outlines, his rigid selection of the most telling darks, and the control he exercises in using only the very minimum of shading, leaving the white of the paper to suggest most of his high lights.

He has a great advantage over many artists who draw architecture, for he is also a most accomplished figure-draughtsman; in his pictures and posters he peoples his market-places and promenades with gay crowds, colourful processions emerge from the doors of his cathedrals, and he has added beauty to his historic buildings by scenes of pageantry. If perspective problems worry you during your early attempts at architectural drawing it would help you to study the rules which govern this subject and which are dealt with on page 82.

FRED
TAYLOR, R.I.

ROBIN HOODS BAY.
June 22

FRED TAYLOR, R.I.

FIGURE DRAWING

Is this the stage for which you have been waiting? If so, it is a splendid plan, before you start to sketch from a model, to study yourself in a glass.

Punch's advice to those about to get married—*don't!* is about the first thing to say to you who are eager to make your first serious drawing from life. A big "*don't.*" First start with observation—*look*—till you see something that no one has seen before. For no one can make *your* discoveries. You must make them yourself!

OBSERVATION

AND COMPARISON

Observation is finding out. Find out, for all you are worth, the mystery and the meaning of your body, if you want to be able to draw well.

This first real look should impress you for the rest of your life. If you have the courage not to draw at all, the first day, it will probably do you much more good than anything else.

Look at yourself then — as you have probably never looked before. The knowledge you gain from an hour's self-study, of a concentrated intense kind, will be a revelation to you.

You want to draw what you know and *feel*, not only just what you see; *look*—before you leap!

Cultivate the *acting* feeling.

The want of *art*—from beginning to end—is *life*. From first to last the want is apparent. It is wanting in the artist himself, in his imagination, form and colour. It comes chiefly from one reason, that he did not *begin* right.

Dress is the clothing of the body, the body is the clothing of the bone; more than that, the body is the clothing of the soul.

Get as near to nature as you can. Study the nude first. Strip off every shred of disguise, and see how your body is hung, how you balance, how you maintain the central gravity, how you get swing and sway of figure, how the arms turn on a pivot; and study, for all you are worth, the feeling of poise, balance, ebb and flow and sway.

Watch your chest expanding, your muscles dilating. After you have studied the general poise and balance of the body, observe the parts—head, hands, feet, legs, trunk, muscles— soaking the actual form into the mind.

Note the ear in relation to the eye, and so on. Watch the

head lifted and lowered and moved from left to right. See what advantage there is in moving the head with the body, or vice versa, and how, as the centre of the body moves there is a corresponding sympathetic action of other parts with it.

Stand up to your work. Sitting is indulgent and lazy, if you are physically fit; and you only get a sitting view. A standing one represents a mastery, manliness, a readiness for action and movement. After all, we are men and women first rather than scribblers, and it may actually be a disgrace to be an artist if you don't do justice to yourself and the powers which are your own personal possesssion.

When you employ a model, make him show, by varied poses, what balance is. Make him lie, make him kneel, make him sit. Now stand up for him, and let him pose you. Send him away, and, with your mind, fill the place he was in; then compare. Now study the model as a mental being. Hand him a funny story to read, and watch him smile, make him frown, sneer, cry, shout, pray, wink, sleep. And "him" applies equally to "her".

The ideal way would be to carry out this plan *before you begin to draw*, and to spend a day or two—perhaps a week—thinking the thing out. You would thus have learned something to last you for all time.

As you pass in the street, or wherever you go, compare every type you meet, and try gradually to compose an ideal from actual observation.

You can go further, if you like, and mentally "place" the type of each person you see. One man is like a horse, another a sheep, another a rabbit, another a cow, and so on; and in an extraordinary way you will often find that these qualities are in the character as well. It will not hurt you to know something about phrenology, or psychology.

Truth is stranger than fiction, and you need the living model; but you must equally be independent of it if you are to *create* (which is the end of Art), especially if you are to have something in your life-study beyond the dull, dreary lines of a weary model.

In drawing the human figure in line you have, again, nothing but three types of line to work with—the straight, bent, and curved.

You will find that you will draw a child best by a series of shapes approximating to the circle. The woman, who comes next, is a series of curves. The man, who comes next, is more

D

or less a series of angles—straight lines, bent lines, crooked lines.

As drawing is measurement, and it is more difficult to measure accurately with curves or circles, begin your work with the straight line, or very nearly straight, always having in mind the eventual curve it must take.

In analysing the proportions of a male figure we usually adopt the standards of ideal beauty which were set by the inspired Greek sculptors, who have, incidentally, provided us with the "Antiques" to be found in every well-equipped art school.

The Greeks considered a small head a sign of beauty, and they usually divided their idealised figures into eight head-lengths. There has been a tendency in modern Art to reduce this ideal proportion to a type of figure seven-and-a-half heads in length; in fact, the generality of British types are seven heads, or even six-and-a-half heads high, so many figures having inordinately long bodies and disproportionately short legs.

For working purposes, however, you should always consider that a standing male figure divided into eight heads is a reasonable standard to work upon.   (See diagram 45)

I have already given you some instruction as to how proportions may be measured by means of a pencil held at arm's length, but here again is a note of the system to be adopted in analysing figure proportion.

Stand about eight feet away from your model.

Hold your pencil upright, with your arm outstretched towards the model. Let the top of your pencil remain steady between your eye and the top of the model's head. Then move your thumb down to the portion of the pencil against which his chin shows. This is obviously your first head length—by which the other proportions can be checked.

Still holding your pencil in position, and your arm stiff, proceed to the other measurements of the figure.

You will find that the second head-length should extend from the chin to a little above the level of the nipples.

The third length should reach from this point to the waist line, slightly below the elbow joint.

The fourth length should end at the lowest portion of the trunk, on a line with the wrist when the arm is held straight down at the side.

MEASUREMENT BY "HEADS"

So you will see that the head and trunk are practically divided into four divisions, the head being one-fourth.

The fifth division reaches to the centre of the thigh, the sixth to the point just below the knee, the seventh slightly below the calf, leaving the final "head" to be taken up by the depth from calf to sole.

These, you should note, are classical proportions.

Measuring from the top of the average arm to the tips of the fingers, you will find the length to be about three heads and a quarter. The upper part takes one-and-a-half heads; the remainder one-and-three-quarters.

The leg is about four heads long, from the socket of the thigh bone—just under the hip—to the heel, and it is divided in the centre by the knee joint.

We shall deal with the proportions of the head in our next lesson. I do not want to confuse you by too many details during your first acquaintance with the figure, when your time should be occupied with general study of the figure as a whole—but it is interesting to notice that the length of the face is usually identical with the length of the hand.

You will find that almost every model varies slightly, but if you memorise these broad facts of proportion—they are not a bit difficult to grasp if you study a living model with our diagram—and familiarise yourself with these measuring points, they will help you to get reasonable proportions, not only into your present life studies, but into imaginary figures later.

The centre of the normal standing figure will be at the middle of the lowest part of the trunk —between the legs. These two halves are divided again exactly, in the upper part at the nipple and in the lower part at the knee.

Another simple measurement can be obtained by dividing the trunk—from its lowest point to the top of the head—into three parts. These parts are divided by the collar bones and the waist line. In a female figure the centre division must be a little smaller than the other two.

You will realise the necessity of knowing something about the general proportions and measurements of the figure, and it will save you time if you consider these questions *before* you attempt your preliminary sketches of the model.

45. RELATIVE PROPORTIONS OF MAN, WOMAN AND CHILD

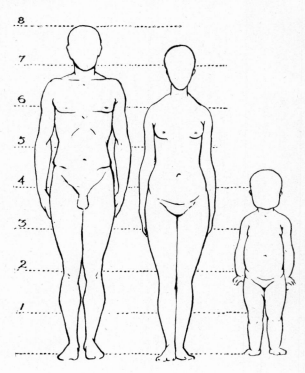

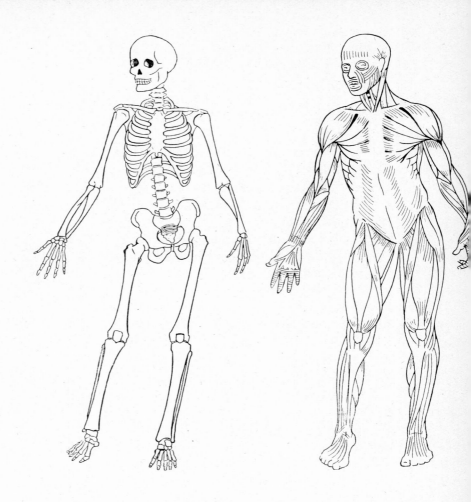

YOUR FIRST
FIGURE
DRAWING

Above we have two explanatory diagrams of the bony structure of the figure, and of the more important surface muscles. The poses are identical, so that you can trace the relation of bone to muscle quite easily. Study of the bony forms is specially important, for where the bones come to the surface at the shoulders, wrists and ankles, they provide you with valuable landmarks in setting up the drawing.

Opposite are three diagrams illustrating a principle of construction in three logical phases, which, by now, should be very familiar to you. I introduced it in the first lesson, and promised that it would be referred to again in more ambitious problems.

The stages are self explanatory, but I would remind you that the first stage demonstrates the first sweep of the life lines; the second—which would, in your drawing, be made over the first—is a more accurate shaping or blocking-in of

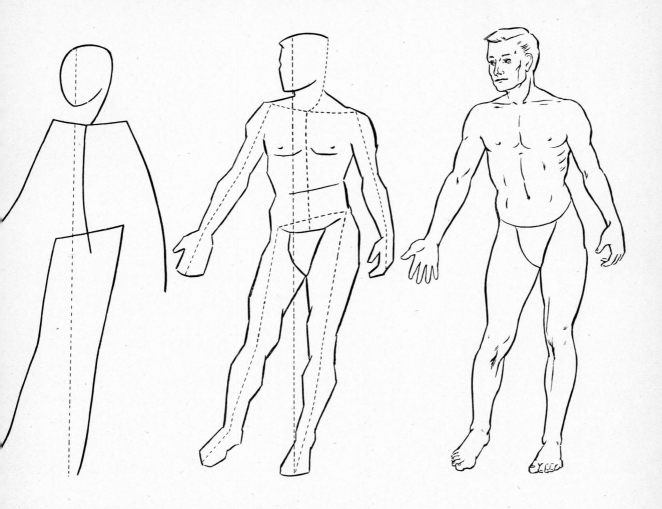

the main masses; and the third stage is a closer representation of the actual appearance of the pose, in simple outlines. In your next lesson you'll be shown how to give more realism to the forms by shading.

Pose the model in a good light, and let him stand about eight paces from you. If you are too close to him you will have difficulty in seeing the figure as a whole.

If you have obtained a satisfactory model, you are lucky; but if you have not persuaded anyone to pose, do not despair, for you ought to discover a highly intelligent and enthusiastic substitute in your own figure reflected from a mirror.

If you pose yourself, try to get a glass long enough to reflect all of your figure. A glass four feet by two should be just right. You can place the mirror on a chair, or stand it against the wall, with base on the floor.

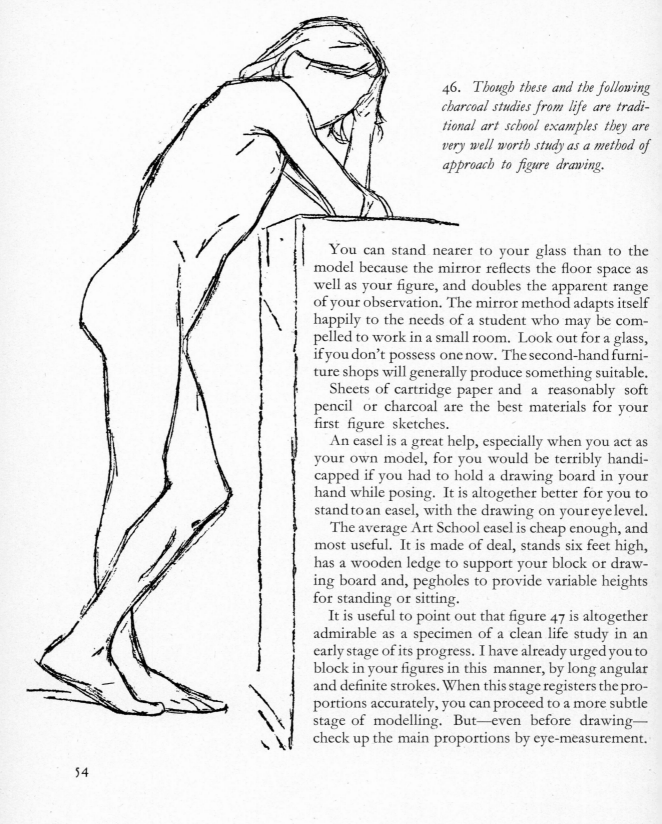

46. Though these and the following charcoal studies from life are traditional art school examples they are very well worth study as a method of approach to figure drawing.

You can stand nearer to your glass than to the model because the mirror reflects the floor space as well as your figure, and doubles the apparent range of your observation. The mirror method adapts itself happily to the needs of a student who may be compelled to work in a small room. Look out for a glass, if you don't possess one now. The second-hand furniture shops will generally produce something suitable.

Sheets of cartridge paper and a reasonably soft pencil or charcoal are the best materials for your first figure sketches.

An easel is a great help, especially when you act as your own model, for you would be terribly handicapped if you had to hold a drawing board in your hand while posing. It is altogether better for you to stand to an easel, with the drawing on your eye level.

The average Art School easel is cheap enough, and most useful. It is made of deal, stands six feet high, has a wooden ledge to support your block or drawing board and, pegholes to provide variable heights for standing or sitting.

It is useful to point out that figure 47 is altogether admirable as a specimen of a clean life study in an early stage of its progress. I have already urged you to block in your figures in this manner, by long angular and definite strokes. When this stage registers the proportions accurately, you can proceed to a more subtle stage of modelling. But—even before drawing— check up the main proportions by eye-measurement.

A word, at this point, as to the method of holding the pencil, in life drawing. Do not, when sketching at the easel and standing, grip your pencil as if you were writing. Hold it with the tips of your first and second fingers and the thumb —practically in the same way as the conductor of an orchestra holds his baton.   Use charcoal, if you prefer it.

Keep your wrist supple, and try also to draw with a sweep of the arm from the elbow and the shoulder.

Your first lines will, of necessity, be very experimental. Try to make them constructive. Drawing begins with the first mark put on the paper, and each succeeding mark must relate properly to the first one.

Do not press too heavily on the pencil at first. You may wish to remove a faulty line, and that won't be easy if the lead has ploughed a furrow in the surface of the paper. You must, incidentally, pay respect to the pencil as a medium, and the best technique is reticent.   (Charcoal dusts off easily!)

Make certain that you can get the entire figure on the paper. We all know the student who, carried away by enthusiasm for the head, draws it so large that before he has completed three-quarters of the figure he finds himself dangerously near

47. Simplification. Registering the main proportions accurately before proceeding to detail or modelling.

55

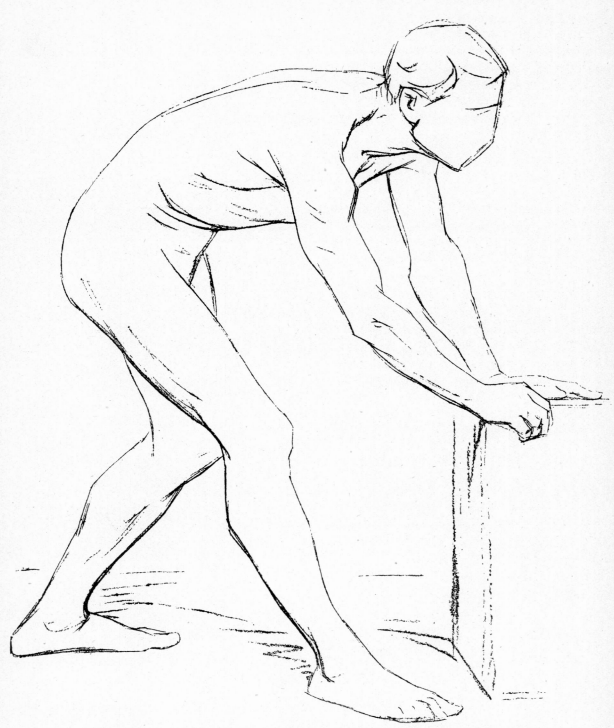

48. *Accurate construction, fluent confident line and simple emphasis, in charcoal.*

the bottom of the paper, and, to be sure of getting in everything at all costs, reduces the legs until the result looks like a portrait of a grotesque dwarf. That could have been avoided by preliminary eye-and-pencil measurement.

Figure 48, a particularly artistic and sensitive life drawing. Though it is practically in outline, it represents the three-dimensional quality—the sense of thickness or throughness —with splendid success. Note especially the sympathetic variety of line, the delicate outlines used to suggest those sides of the figure on which the light falls, and the appreciation of form and modelling shown on the shadow sides.

If we look at the pose from the point of view of the mass presented by the whole—as discussed earlier in the lesson— we shall see that the legs and feet below the knees form a rough triangle, and that there is another in the upper part, continued along the line of the back to an apex in the region of the top of the head.

In measuring up this model the artist noticed that the point of the chin came exactly over the front of the right foot, while the centre of the body—that portion which meets the top of the right thigh—is exactly over the front of the other foot. You should observe such coincidences in your models. Now let us consider the details of the figure.

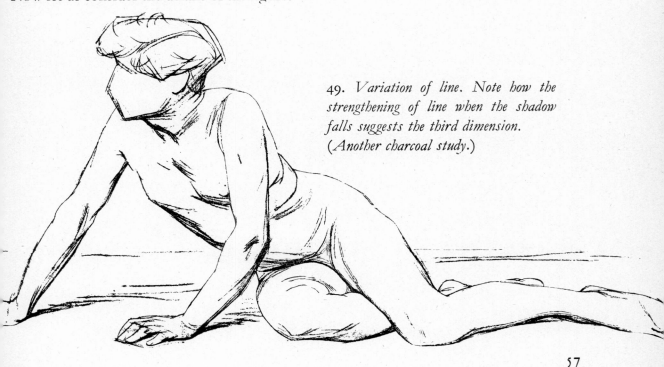

49. *Variation of line. Note how the strengthening of line when the shadow falls suggests the third dimension. (Another charcoal study.)*

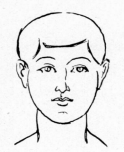
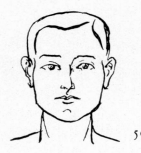

50

Diagrams 50 and 51 remind you that a man's head is squarer than a woman's both in front and side views. In profile the head nearly fits into a square; a man's head more so than a woman's, which is rather more oval, on an axis from the chin to the top back of the skull.

Diagram 52 shows the proportions of the head and face. The eyes fall on a line which practically divides the total

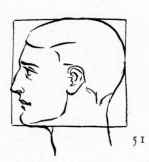

51

depth of the head. If the *face* is divided into three, the first dividing line gives the position of the eye-brows and the top of the ears; the second, the bottom of the nose and the bottom of the ears. On dividing the lowest "third" into three, the first line gives the position of the mouth the second the top of the chin.

The distance between the eyes is the width of one eye, so

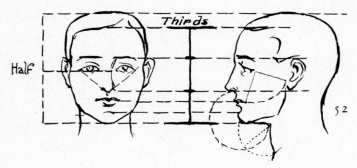

52

Diagrams by a pupil.

58

the distance between the outer corners of the eyes is equal to three "eye-lengths." Again, lines drawn from the corners of the eyes to the bottom of the nose should form a right-angle. The distance from the bottom of the nose to the bottom of the chin—one-third the face length—is equal to the length from the point of the chin to the top of the throat, and of the length of the throat to the top of the breast-bone.

Figures 53 and 54, showing heads in various poses, indicate how a head should first be sketched in.

Life lines again!

When the oval of the head is roughed in, a line is drawn down its centre—in full face—and on this a cross line drawn at right angles, at half the depth of the head, gives the position of the eyes.

Another cross line is drawn to mark the top of the face, and the distance between this and the bottom of the chin is divided into three parts, the lines of these divisions giving the positions of the eye-brows, nose, and ears. When the head is raised or lowered, these cross lines should be drawn in curves which follow the roundness of the head, and give the relative position of the ears. In three-quarter view the line drawn through the centre of the face must follow the curve of the profile.

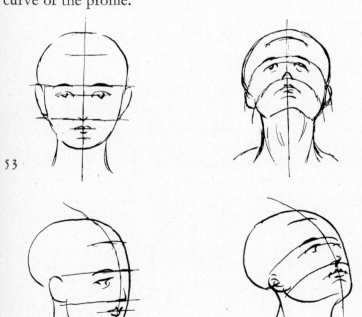

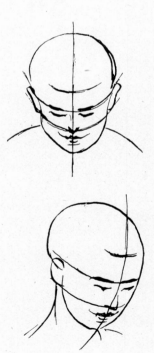

53

54

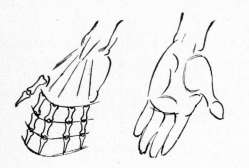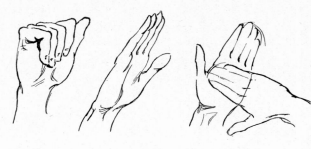

HANDS AND FEET The hand is one of the most difficult parts of the human figure to draw; and it is equally difficult to give any definite method of drawing it.

The first diagram shows the general "scaffolding" of the wrist and hand—giving the lines of tendons from the wrist to the thumb and fingers, and the position of the knuckles. The second diagram shows the prominent masses on the palm of a hand. A hand is generally the same length as the face. The length of the fingers is about equal to the width of the palm. The distance from the wrist to the knuckles is equal to the distance from the latter to the tip of the middle finger.

Very few students realise the importance of the hands in the suggestion of character. You'll find that the character of your model, the shape of his or her body, and even the prevailing emotions, is expressed—one might almost say concentrated—in the hands. You don't see a fat man with long fingers. A brutal type, with ugly irregular features and a thick ungainly body, will have a correspondingly clumsy hand. A tall, slender figure will offer you long gracefully tapering fingers.

Now as to the construction of the hand. Perhaps the first fact you'll appreciate is the feeling of radiation in the fingers. The first undirected glance may perhaps suggest that the palm of the hand is a piece of flesh with the fingers sticking out at one end like pegs; but look again—and you'll see that the real construction of the fingers begins somewhere in the region of the wrist. Draw four long lines from the wrist, spreading them in a fan shape to suggest the fingers, and you'll have a reasonable basis on which to build a more sincere drawing.

The thumb is more or less independent, and can be drawn so, although it has some connection with this feeling of radiation already seen in the fingers.

Now clench the hand, or get your model to do so, and realise the wedge-like shapes into which the sections of the fingers fall. There are three of these sections, or phalanges, in each finger, and they show a gradual progression of size from the base to the tip. Divide the hand into two or three broad masses, or shapes, and you'll not find any tremendous difficulties.

The feet. Many students—and artists—fail to make the feet appear to join properly to the leg. The joint can only be expressed well if the anatomy of the ankle is realised, and the lines of the ankle-bones run on into the foot. Points to be particularly noted are that the inner ankle-bone is *higher* than the outer, and that the flatness of the heel and sole runs, on the *outer* part of the foot, to the little toes. But there is a distinct hollow on the *inside* of the foot between the heel and the ball of the big toe.

In drawing the inside of a foot the line of the ankle can be run on to the ball of the big-toe while, in representing a back view of the foot, the Achilles tendon should be run right down to the heel.

Do not forget that the heel projects back well beyond the ankle. In savage and coloured races the backward projection of the heel is even more pronounced. My pupil's diagrams illustrate the few special points I have mentioned.

The diagrams on these two pages are by a pupil.

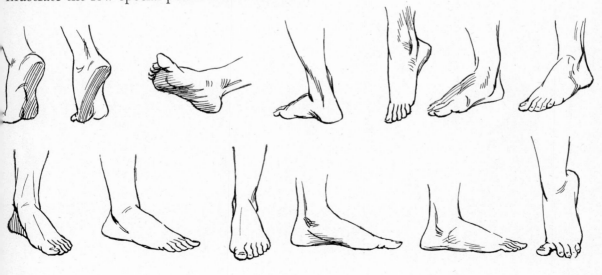

55. *Further diagrams by pupils.*

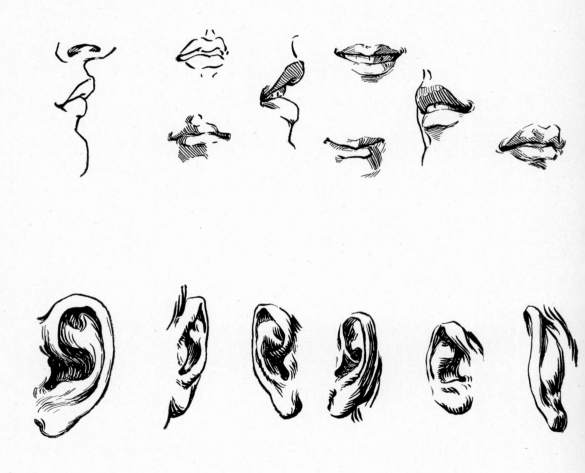

The Eye. First a section of the eye. The shaded portion emphasises the fact that the lids are quite thick, and this is a point which should always be remembered. The thickness of the lids can be seen in the various sketches of eyes.

Next we have a general rough diagram of an eye showing important lines which must nearly always be represented. The little tear duct, at the inner corner of the eye, is an important detail, and should always be represented, even in small pen-and-ink sketches.

Most students go to pieces in the drawing of the eye in profile. Remember the globe-like form and also that the lids, when you draw them, must project a sufficient distance *beyond* the front of the eye to suggest their *thickness* and to indicate that there is room for them to close comfortably over the eyeball.

The Mouth is capable of the greatest expression, and the mobility of the lips is a fact that should be constantly borne in mind; the corners of the mouth as compared with the centre should be carefully noted. It will be found usually that, in repose, the corners are always lower than the centre. These illustrations should indicate to the painstaking student the lines of study.

The Ear. The most important thing to remember about the ear is exactly how it is set on to the head. If you feel along your cheek to the ear you will notice that the cheek-bone or "zygomatic arch" ends at the ear. You can study this from the skull and will find the tiny orifice of the ear in the bony structure. The ear is largely cartilaginous, but the lobe is soft; the position of the "helix" and "anti-helix" (the names given by anatomists to the curly structures) should be carefully studied, and you should note also the small triangular shape where the ear "fits on" to the head.

And now we come to diagrams of *the nose* on this page.

The nose needs great study. You will observe, if you look carefully, that parts of the nose look hard and parts not so hard; where the bony structure is suggested under the skin, the nose naturally looks harder than the portion containing the nostrils, which are more cartilaginous, or gristly and fleshy. The placing of the nostrils demands great attention and the various small planes which exist in a well-chiselled nose should be studied carefully.

Figure 56 shows roughly the planes of the nose and mouth and the relative position of the eye.

56

It will, I think, encourage you if I stand aside for a while and let one of my pupils talk to you about his methods of tackling the types of study which I set him. I gave him lessons by post while he was stationed in Burma and he produced these studies while he was on leave and working in Paris.

"All the poses on the opposite page involve a realisation of action *and* construction," he explains, "and this is how I proceed with such sketches:

"Take the third study—of the seated figure, beneath the first dancing model. In this third subject, the first thing to do, as usual, was to realise the *pose* — in about five minutes.

"The model's head is thrown back, and the inner ends of the eye-brow, eye and nostrils are more or less in a horizontal line. The mouth is below the left nostril, and the end of the chin below that.

"I rapidly put in these details, then the line of the right jaw was swept down till it met the 'bonnet string' muscle, which ran into the collar bone. The left side of the throat started upwards from the inner side of the collar bone, and was drawn in, and this enabled me to find the position of the left cheek, bonnet-string muscle, and collar bone. I followed this by marking the hollow beneath this left collar bone, and indicating the wall of the left chest, and the swelling of the upper part of the breast. Then back to the right side, where the outer part of the collar bone, and its continuation of the deltoid were drawn. The next step was to draw the lines indicating the curve of the right wall of the chest, the inner line of the arm, and the breast.

"I then finished the inner line of the right arm, and the side of the body, to the crease which is caused by the lower ribs, and returned to the left side, where the shoulder and deltoid outline was sketched in. Then the under line of the breast was roughly shaded, and the line of the chest to the swelling caused by the line of the lower ribs.

"I had kept in view the life line given by the breast-bone, and its continuation to the umbilicus and fork, and now sketched this in. Using it as a guide, the shading of the abdominal muscles were indicated, and *not till then* the *outline* of the waist and hips were drawn; so on down the legs.

"You will notice, therefore, that I built my structure round an imaginary life line, noting solidity and pose at the same

Quick action sketches by a pupil.

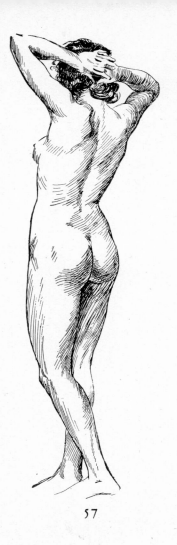

57

THE COMPLETE

FIGURE

IN PEN-AND-INK

time. I didn't, as many students do, merely make an 'outline diagram' of the figure. I first felt for the anatomical forms, and then *based my outline on them*. By this means form and proportion were realised together, and this inevitably included *Action*. For example, the shading of the strap muscle of the stretched-out right leg, running into the outline of the lower thigh, was drawn before the outline of the inner upper thigh.

"All the lightning pencil sketches on the same page followed a similar principle.

"As I had little more than five minutes for any one of the poses, you mustn't be too critical."

I liked these quick sketches so much that I asked the pupil to send me some pen-sketches based on my lessons. These are the notes which accompanied his work:

"The quickest sketch is that drawn in the top right hand corner opposite." (Figure 59.) "It was done in two minutes, and has sufficient detail to enable one to make a finished drawing from it. The positions of the principal constructional details were first indicated in pencil, and the sketch completed with a pen; the lines, you will find, are delicate on the light sides, and heavier where there is shadow, and the direction of the lines of shading follow the form.

"Figure [58] was a five-minute sketch in pencil, inked in during the five-minutes rest, and shows how valuable a quick sketch can be. Note that though the left thigh is nearly pure outline, it manages to suggest the rotundity of the limb.

"The other sketches (Figures 57 and 60) were done in the 25-minute poses. They are rather more carefully drawn, for there was more time to work and this enabled one to find the correct direction for the lines of shading, so that they give the best indication of form. Crosshatch was only used where it was necessary.

"In the back-view figure (60) one sees, I hope, the value of slight indications of anatomical form in the correct place to give life to the drawing.

"I used always to sit 12 to 15 feet away, so that the model appeared to fill the paper I was drawing on. (The figures were drawn between 8 and 9 inches high.) I faced the model direct, the paper being held with its top edge close to the

PEN DRAWINGS BY A PUPIL SHOWING
HOW CONSTRUCTION, TEXTURE AND
LIGHT AND SHADE CAN BE REPRESENTED
IN SIMPLE, NATURAL LINE.

model's feet; so that when I glanced from the model to the paper, I held a sort of photographic image of the model filling the sheet of paper. And I endeavoured to hold this first photographic impression by memory, while I drew in the details, and this kept the *action* of the original pose.

"The poses were nearly all in strained positions which could not be held for long, and usually, by the end of the period, had altered considerably, for the arms or legs tired and drooped, or the twisted body swung towards the normal. For this reason it was usually hopeless to start by blocking in the whole figure, and then drawing in the detail later; for, by the time one had blocked in the legs, the head, shoulders and arms had moved, and the lines that blocked them in were useless. There was no time to waste on corrections, if one wanted to indicate the anatomical details to give form.

"Then, as 'blocking in' would not answer, I built up the drawing anatomically—that is, 'feeling' the way by following the essential forms, and balancing them by drawing them in *alternately* on each side of the Life Line of Action. This enabled me to sketch the Form and put in the shading at the same time; in fact the shading was part of the Form.

"This is not so difficult as it sounds, and practice made it easier and easier."

My pupils give me continual proof of the truth of that comforting final statement.

DRAPERY Always study folds of clothing carefully before drawing them. Every crease is caused by the figure and limbs inside the clothes creating a tension at one part and a relaxation at the opposite side; so try to visualize the limbs and their forms under the clothing. If you do this properly you will always keep your figures in correct proportion.

It is very good practice to draw the nude figure, and fit clothes to it; or, vice versa, to make a tracing of a costume study, and draw the nude figure inside the clothing. Drapery, if it is to express the existence of the limb beneath, or its action, cannot be drawn "anyhow." First of all, you have got to realise the shape and action which causes the folds to fall in certain directions. Then you need to consider the character and substance of the material you are representing, for, quite obviously, a heavy cloth will fall in much simpler and more solid folds than cotton and silk.

Drapery is a subject which really does need a sense of selection. If you introduce every trivial mark and wrinkle on the surface of clothes, you confuse the bigger lines. Look out particularly, in drawing a human figure, for the folds of the drapery at the armpits, elbows and knees. Don't get into the habit of sticking in two or three conventional lines which you think may be "good enough" to express action—the sort of "broad-arrow" markings you may have seen in very rough comic drawings.

Here is a very vigorous and confident outline drawing of clothing by a pupil.

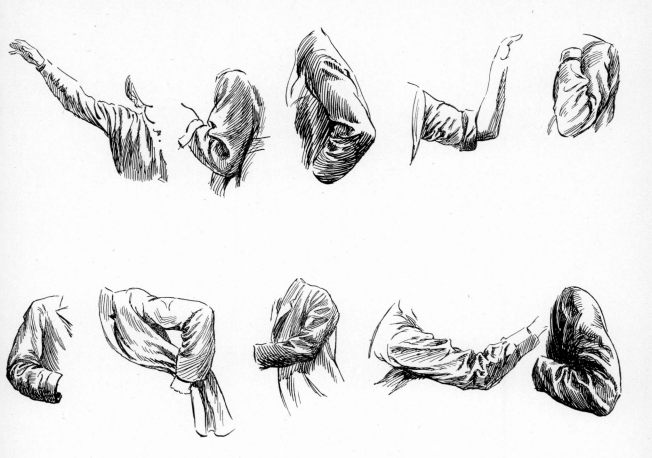

61. *A selection of more conventional studies by another pupil, who submitted them solely as conscientious diagrams and* not *as examples of quality of line.*

  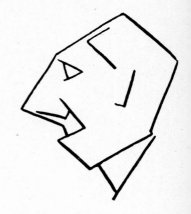

HUMOROUS DRAWING

ONE OF THE happiest advantages which result from a know-ledge of figure drawing is that it enables you to make sketches of quaint types and characters whom you may encounter, and to give expression to your sense of humour. A very large number of my pupils have discovered that caricature and character-drawing are both pleasant and profitable, and many leading humorous artists have given them the benefit of their advice, which has been incorporated in my lessons.

I feel that, at this stage, it may be a great pleasure to you to share some of the help which has proved so invaluable as an introduction to the fascinating world of humorous drawing. Let us, then, glance at the methods of such outstanding pic-torial comedians as Alfred Leete, "Fougasse," Bert Thomas, Tom Webster and H. M. Bateman.

ALFRED LEETE The late Alfred Leete introduced my pupils to a very in-dividual method of observation and analysis of character—which you can test, when next you are in a bus, tram, or train by studying your fellow passengers. You may perhaps find, seated in the corner, an obviously shy little man, with a "sur-prised" look on his face—raised eyebrows, and a wondering, nervous expression. That surprised line you will be able to trace all through his face. It is not only in his eyes and eye-brows, but in his quaint little mouth, in his chin, in the shape of his head—everywhere.

Sitting next to him may be one of those chunky, hefty persons, with a broad, "stubby" nose, deep-set eyes, power-ful, determined expression. That "stubby" line is everywhere

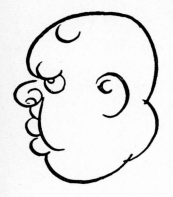  

about him. It is his characteristic—his "line." Whatever your other types may be like, you will discover that they have their characteristic line. The sharp, bird-like, hatchet-faced man is not only sharp in the nose, but angular in line throughout; the aggressive bull-dog sort of person is "bull-doggy" all over —in every line of him; the fat, lumpy, saggy, over-fed old gentleman is full of rolling, greedy lines. Leete's drawings on these two pages show you clearly what he meant.

It is a remarkable thing that, once you have hit upon a man's characteristic line, you will find that he continues it even in the smaller details of his clothes. You will discover that the fat man almost invariably wears the only type of collar which he could wear to make his study complete—and that the thin, angular man, who is a series of acute lines and sharp points, wears a sharp-pointed collar. The fat, blobby, pendulous person is exactly represented by fat blobby lines —a series of short, lumpy curves—and so on.

Observation on these lines can always be the most fascinating hobby. An ordinary walk along the street, the inevitable wait on a railway station for an overdue train, the hanging about for that friend who is always late, should become an entertainment instead of a bore.

The brilliant work of "Fougasse," Art Editor of *Punch*, who I am proud to claim as one of my old pupils, has reduced figure-drawing to the quaintest and simplest of formulas, which, coupled with a very individual sense of humour has brought him a unique reputation. He has developed a kind of pictorial shorthand which, relying on the reader's own imagination, contrives to deliver a wonderfully complete message—often without any explanatory letterpress. He

FOUGASSE

71

FOUGASSE

maintains that his work depends on humour rather than art —but—don't you envy the wonderful simplicity of his line, and the almost magical way in which it has told so many humorous "stories" in *Punch*?

He does not enjoy expressing his "views" on humour and art, but he is too generous to refuse an opportunity to help my students, and this is what he said when I asked him for a few words for you:

"I think there is one thing in our work which is often overlooked. And that is, that we are able to make the greatest use of the readers' own imagination. He will often, for instance, recall with enjoyment the expression on a face in some drawing he has liked, whereas in actual fact the face, as drawn, consisted merely of a dot for the mouth, and a dash for the eyebrow. The expression, and the face itself, really existed in the reader's own imagination, which filled in all the blanks, probably better than the artist would have done. The production of a humorous idea by pictorial means is, to me, really a type of shorthand—which uses symbols that we have come to recognise as signifying certain things. My ideas seldom come from anything I've *seen*. I don't lift subjects from real life."

And yet, as you'll realise from the little marginal sketches which "Fougasse" did for me, these types, in spite of their economy of line, are ridiculously realistic. We have seen all these people, they have an individuality that does not depend on traditional comic tricks, they don't remind us of other humorous artists, and although we are, by now, happily familiar with his "shorthand"—with that astonishing economy of line which suggests character and movement—he always gives us something to think about.

And now, let us look at the work of Bert Thomas; a man who does depend on realism. Having realised the remarkable sense of character in his studies you will perhaps be puzzled by their technique. Bert Thomas explains it:

"I have had many enquiries about my "broken lines," chalk effects, etc. There is no secret about them. *You* can draw with broken lines if you work on a Whatman surface, and use a spikey old brush as I do. There is not the slightest reason in the world why you should not use it with quite as much facility; but the great point is, what are you going to *say*? What's the message you are going to deliver with its aid? Tricks are nothing. The thought you want to express is everything. You were born with an individuality that neither I nor any other living artist can use. Remember that fact—that you have a chance to say something that nobody else on earth can say—in *your* way."

"I can't repeat too definitely that manual dexterity counts simply for nothing. You have probably got quite as clever a *hand* as some of the biggest artists who ever lived. Your fingers can do exactly the same work. Where a genius differs from the ordinary person is in *brain*, and that is what you want to develop. The brain will control the hand very thoroughly, in time, if you train it properly."

He is often asked, "What are your methods of caricature? Do you look for outstanding peculiarities in a man and exaggerate those until the result is funny? Do you look for definite comic points? Have you any system of observing these?"

The answer is that he doesn't look for "comic" anything —and emphatically not for "comic points." If he did, it would be so very easy to give a big-nosed man an elephant's trunk, or a big-mouthed man the facial characteristics of the crocodile. He advises you not to be carried away by comparatively unimportant facial peculiarities or minor mannerisms. Try to sum up the *bigger* facts.

Artists need practice, as a discipline for their professional appearances—quite as much as musicians and singers do. They get stale, mannered and dull when they don't practise their scales and five-finger exercises daily. One of Bert's hobbies is the drawing of familiar objects in unfamiliar positions; it's very useful as a test of draughtsmanship and as an artistic tonic. He uses a mirror for posing himself, if he wants to verify little details, but relies for most of his work on a well-stocked memory, and observation. He roughs out humorous or other drawings in charcoal or pencil, and almost always inks them in with a matted wreck of a brush, which has grown stiff and spikey with clogged ink, and which somehow he finds the most responsive and useful of drawing tools.

In these few pages I shall only be able to give you the briefest introduction to a fascinating subject which will, I hope, add greatly to your interest in drawing. But I want you to realise that a knowledge of figure construction, and study *from life* is a necessary foundation for success in humorous art; and I hope it will encourage you to know that many of the most popular pictorial humorists of today built their careers on the principles which this book outlines.

BERT THOMAS

73

INMAN

TOM WEBSTER

H. M. BATEMAN

If, by chance, you are interested in sport, and would like to try the type of sketch which made Tom Webster the most successful contributor to *The Daily Mail* for many years, let us consider his methods.

One could quote numberless instances of the fact that Webster invariably discovered a new point of view from which to record every sports function. An England and Scotland match was recorded by Tom, completely, by the feathers in the bonnets of Scottish spectators. If England scored, the feathers curled up in depression. When Scotland took the lead, the feathers would be triumphantly cocksure.

In discussing that caricature of Inman, he said this: "Caricaturing Inman is something more than putting a big nose over a thin protruding upper lip. I went to a billiards championship every day for five weeks, and in that period I must have drawn at least two hundred sketches of Inman. He would play so faultlessly that one had to look hard for humour—and to tell the story of his genius by other means. I found it in the pattern of his opponent's trousers, in such an apparent trifle as a puff of smoke blown across the table, in the restlessness of a visitor, the voice of the marker—in other things utterly apart from the man and his skill."

Yes, in Tom Webster's work, a remarkable originality of idea was certainly combined with a fluent technique.

Now let us turn to the work of that great humorous artist, H. M. Bateman—the extraordinary vitality of whose pen line makes such a perfect complement to, and illustration of, his mental attitude. His line is as incisive as his observation, his vision as sure and instantaneous as his draughtsmanship. It is a common error of the un-initiated to assume that a drawing in a few simple and essential lines is "just dashed off"; that the artist is possessed of some mysterious trick, knack, formula or innate ability which enables him to convey in a few sure strokes what another will achieve (or fail to achieve) by more elaborate methods. Many a student, misled by the apparent ease with which the result is attained, overlooks the obvious fact that it is easier to express oneself elaborately than pithily.

Bateman uses his sketchbooks everywhere, and many people, even his best friends, on looking through these books, seem astonished at the range of subjects which have interested him. The simple explanation is that *everything* interests him—such apparently uninteresting things as weighing machines, motors, coal-carts, sewing machines, ploughs and bicycles, or any other forms of mechanism. You may look in vain through his sketch books for comic drawings.

Discussing that drawing, "*Not so dusty!*" he said, "It amused me to do it, and I do think I have managed to get these chaps dripping wet. They are emphatically types I have remembered. I am equally sure you must have seen them. They are everywhere, and I made this drawing because it happened to be a crisp little picture with a crisp little joke." Isn't it an object lesson in expressive line? And do not the other caricatures by Bateman give evidence of his supreme talent as a humorous artist?

" 'ow's things ? "
" Not so dusty "

H. M. BATEMAN

H. M. BATEMAN

ANIMAL DRAWING

Good drawing is chiefly a matter of *seeing* correctly, and of discliplining and training the eye in the art of knowing what to look for.

The art critic of *The Tailor and Cutter*, for instance, who goes to the Academy each year to see how many buttons the artists have omitted from their sitters' coats, cannot be said to have the eye of an artist.

You must train yourself to look at things broadly if you want to be able to draw the forms of things; no amount of attention to small details will compensate for the loss of the larger outlook; and in order to learn to draw animals, we shall find two things vitally necessary—patience and speed; patience first, for this quality is needed in order to commit most of what we see to memory.

When we try to catch such an action as that of a cat washing itself, we must get down, as quickly as possible, something like this sketch below—noting, that the left leg is supporting and pushing forward the shoulder, which enables the cat to get its head far enough round to lick the right shoulder. The right leg, being thrust forward and used as a balance, rises occasionally off the ground with the movement; when it is resting on the ground, only the outer edge touches the ground, as we realise from the fact that the under-surface is showing.

This is a long explanation to give of so simple an action, and yet you will not represent the details on paper properly without this amount of thought.

Contrast this little note, in imagination, with a photograph which may have been taken of identically the same pose. You will find that the camera, being quicker than the eye, has arrested the action "dead," so that the cat looks more or less as if it were cast in bronze instead of being a lithe, living thing, capable of assuming a totally different action a fraction of a second later.

Always remember that, in portraying an action, you must suggest both what has immediately preceded it, as well as what will happen after. You will find this truth exemplified

HOW TO LOOK
AT ANIMALS

SKETCH BY
WARWICK REYNOLDS

in all good Art. You can only gain the power to express action, "off your own bat" and directly, from study of nature; but you can always get plenty of opportunity at a Zoological Gardens—or around your own home—to study animals in repose. When your drawing is interrupted by the animal getting up or changing its position, start something else.

We are told that the Japanese do not draw directly from animals when studying them, but simply *look*, and when they have looked sufficiently long, they draw them entirely from *memory*. By this means, they are able to *select*—only putting into a drawing what they have retained as absolutely essential and discarding a lot of unnecessary facts which would only tend to overlay or confuse what they wish to express.

Fixity, of course, is abhorred by life, which is fluid and continually in sequence. To draw from a model who is paid carefully to "keep the pose" must develop attitudes which can be kept for a long time so as to be "copied" accurately. Too much of this cannot be beneficial, and there is no doubt that more "live" studies could often be made from the people round about one, who are not keeping a pose.

One of the joys of animal-drawing is that it forces one to become decisive and alert in noting things.

In drawing an animal in action, I have always a pre-disposition to get in the backbone first because everything is hung from this, as it were.

Also, observation *before* one commences to draw not only accustoms one to the action, but enables the necessary analysis to be made. This, of course, includes the mental noting of the construction, which has to be realised even in the first slight sketch.

DRAWING BY JOHN SKEAPING
from Animal Drawing (The Studio Publications)

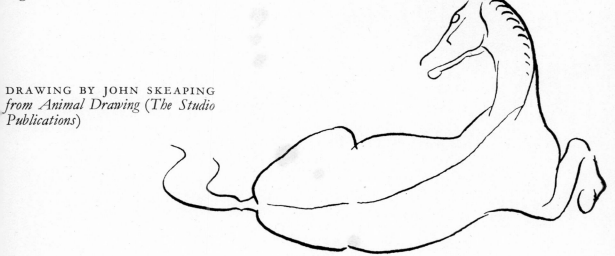

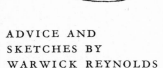

The quick sketch of the mouse, which is illustrated in three stages on this page, will explain "fluidity" more clearly. Let us see how Warwick Reynolds tackled it:

In the first stage, knowing that the backbone controls the whole action, he made a bold sweep for that. Beginning at the nose, the line sweeps back to the spine, only stopping to give the accent of the shoulder, then right on down and out

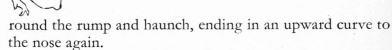

round the rump and haunch, ending in an upward curve to the nose again.

In the next figure the body is balanced, and the action begins to take more definite shape by the addition of the tail, the ears, and the eye-patch, also the furred portion of fore and hind legs.

In the final stage he added the eye and whiskers in black ink, and the feet in pencil outline. Now he mixed a dark

tone of wash (using lamp black), and applied an even tone over the whole of the body, with the exception of the eye-patch and ear.

On the opposite page are some studies of ducks, also by Reynolds. The first being in repose he allowed himself more time for noting it down.

The trained observer of birds and beasts would deduce from this sketch that it shows the bird in winter-time. The wing-feathers are spread out and clapped against its side; one wing is split into three sections, two of which peep from below the left wing, while the third portion is trailing down near the tail; the head is jammed down as far as possible into the shoulders (like a man with coat collar up), and altogether there is a feeling of the feathers being ruffled up for the sake of warmth.

When he had made this sketch in outline, and got all the ground work in, the "local colour" was next set down by indicating the black head, dark wing-coverts and breast, and the direction of the markings on feathers near rump.

The sketch of the duck preening its breast feathers (page 80), was, of course, more rapid. The drawing was started from the feather-creases in the bend of the neck, the line was carried down and round the head, and up again, over the shoulder in a sweep down to the tail, from which the line was again swept up to the neck. The details in the wing-feathers were added subsequently, as there was no time to get them in before the bird shifted.

In looking at a horse's head full-on, its construction at once suggests itself in the form of two diamonds, as in the illustration; the horse's eyes are built on the outer points of the top diamond, the nostrils in the same manner on the lower one, the fore-lock on the topmost one, the mouth on the lowest, the ears being added and the shape of the white marking extending from the forehead to muzzle. A simple tone over the dark portions then completes the drawing.

This diagram is introduced, not because you are expected to draw in these two diamonds every time you do a horse's head in this position, but simply to call your attention to forms which may assist you to draw various animals.

In drawing a lion, tiger or almost any of the cat family full face, an octagon upon an octagon, similar to the diamonds, will give you somewhere near the structure.

When drawing the side view of a pig if you think of a large bean, you will get the whole shape of the body, and the addition of the head and legs will complete the animal.

In most of the fishes, look for the cigar or torpedo shape·
All these things will help you greatly in setting down the
animals.

The general characteristics of most of the deer and ante-
lopes: a prominent feature is the pot-hook swing of the neck
the straight flatness at the top of the shoulders, the rise in the
back, the way the rump protrudes over the hind-quarters,
the knock-kneed tendency of the hind-legs, the way the fore-
legs are set back under the shoulder, the large ears, and, of
course, slender legs and hoofs.

The Otter and the Sea-Lion. Note the blunt wedge-shaped
heads of both, the stiff bristly whiskers, position of the eye,
the smallness and position of the ear, the long neck and body,
the general torpedo-shape adapted to driving through the
water, the powerful fins of the sea-lion replaced in the otter
by the driving force of the tail. Under water the resemblance
is even more marked, and these general observations will
help you when drawing either.

The hippopotamus and crocodile are other
obvious examples of points of resemblance.
Compare animals, and you will discover
many other interesting similarities.

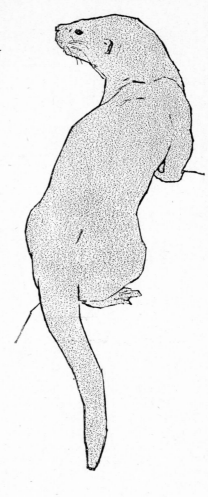

POINTS OF
RESEMBLANCE
BETWEEN
ANIMALS

F

PERSPECTIVE

HORIZONTAL

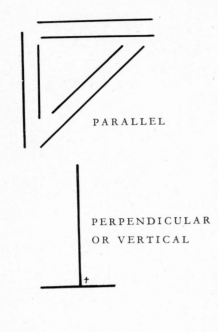

PARALLEL

PERPENDICULAR
OR VERTICAL

INCLINED OR OBLIQUE

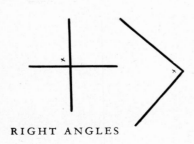

RIGHT ANGLES

THE DIAGRAMS on this and the following pages introduce you—not too abruptly, I hope—to a department of drawing which it is absolutely necessary for you to understand if you wish to represent three-dimensional, or solid, objects convincingly. These preliminary notes will be valuable to you here, especially in drawing architecture.

When we draw anything, we have to represent it on a flat surface—distance and depth have all to be got on one "plane"—such as a sheet of paper or card. This flat surface which we draw on has to represent some objects, say, ten miles away, others five miles away, and still others so close that we can touch them.

If we look through a window, and, standing quite still, trace on the surface of the glass, with our finger or a piece of soap, the objects which we see through the glass, we actually represent them all on one flat plane, whatever distance they may be away. How are we to represent "distance," "depth," "solidity" and "third dimension" in our sketches?

By means of that students' bugbear—*Perspective*.

If you will read these pages carefully, and study the diagrams, I think the main principles of perspective will be clear to you.

Perspective is a derivation of the latin "perspectum," the past participle of the verb "perspicere" which means "to look through." "Perspective," therefore, means "looking through," and in Art refers to the drawing of objects on a flat surface so as to give the picture the same third dimensional effect of depth, distance, solidity as the objects themselves.

It is necessary to discuss the elementary principles of perspective at this stage, and it should be easy to do so in a simple manner. First, it may be useful to explain the meaning of one or two of the *terms* used in perspective.

Horizontal lines are those which are either flat on the ground, or quite level in relation to the ground. For example, a square table stands on the ground and its top is level. The four edges of the top are *each horizontal* lines.

Parallel lines are those which, if extended together in any direction, will remain the same distance apart.

62. *The elementary lines referred to in this chapter.*

63. *Objects receding to a vanishing point.*

Perpendicular or *vertical* lines are those which are exactly upright—at right angles to horizontal lines or to the ground.

Inclined lines are those which are tilted or inclined towards the ground.

Oblique lines are those which slant—which are not perpendicular, parallel or at right angles.

A homely illustration can be given in the statement that the floor of your room is bounded by *horizontal* lines, the top of the wall, where the ceiling commences, forms a *parallel* line with the floor, the walls joining floor to ceiling are *perpendicular* or *vertical*, while the sloping roof of your house is made up of *inclined* lines.

Now, having realised the meaning of these elementary terms, let us consider a few simple rules of perspective.

Look first at the Figure 63. This gives an illustration of the fact that objects appear smaller as they recede from you. This diminution is not haphazard, but in regular progression. Widths decrease as well as heights, therefore lines which are actually parallel in Nature appear to get closer together as they recede, until they actually meet at a point on the horizon which we call the *Vanishing Point*. (Indicated by the letters V.P.)

If we are looking at a level road—such as in this particular diagram—the sides of the road, the telegraph wires and all the level lines which are parallel to the road—such as the roofs of the houses, the telegraph wires, the nearest wall, the kerb stones or the grassy bank—will vanish to the same vanishing point.

The vanishing point will be exactly as high as our eyes. It will always be on a horizontal line, called the horizon, and will move just as we move; if we sit down the horizon will come down too, keeping exactly at our eye level. On the

RULES OF
PERSPECTIVE

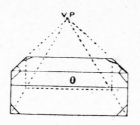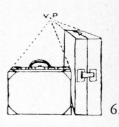

other hand, the higher we mount upward, the higher will the horizon appear. You know how much more you can view of the sea from the top of a cliff than down on the beach by the water's edge.

The use of a horizontal line and vanishing point is necessary in the drawing of the simplest object in perspective, and Figure 64 gives illustrations of objects such as you should easily be able to draw in correct perspective, now that the use of a single vanishing point has been explained to you, and you have realised the principles governing lines which run towards an imaginary horizon.

At first, the fixing of vanishing points where two have to be used may appear a confusing problem, but actually it is comparatively simple if you start properly.

Take, as your model, some simple object such as a box, and place it in a position similar to that shown in my Figure 65, about two yards away from you, and below your eye level. Sit so that you have a wall squarely in front.

We have now to fix the height of your horizon—which, as I have previously explained, is an imaginary line on a level with your eyes—and the position of a definite "point of sight." Look directly in front of you, and choose some object on the wall which will enable you to fix, in your mind, the

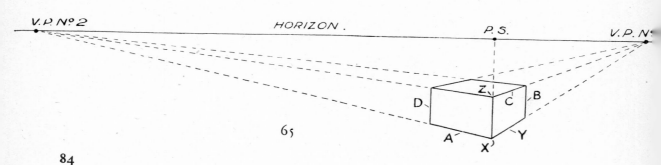

65

height of the eye-level. Imagine the horizon line continued indefinitely along the wall on either side of the object you have fixed. Then draw a horizontal line on your paper representing this.

The next important thing is to fix the position of the base of the nearest edge (X-Z) of the box you are drawing; the base will be the point X and you should get it definitely placed on the paper, fixing its relative distance below the horizon line according to the depth which you wish your drawing to occupy. Having fixed this point X, all your subsequent measurements will be regulated by the distance from X to the horizon line.

Now take an ordinary flat foot-rule, hold it out at arm's length, upright, with the lower portion covering the edge of the box marked X-Z. Observe where the line X-Z, when continued upwards would cross the horizon line. Actually *mark* this point, if you like, by fixing a drawing pin or a little piece of paper on the wall; indicate it also on your drawing with a definite dot and the letters P.S.—point of sight—as shown in our diagram.

Now take your ruler again, and at arm's length follow the apparent direction of the lower edge of the box Y. (A walking stick, or a piece of string held taut, are useful substitutes if you have to check considerable lengths.)

Notice where the continuation of this line Y cuts across the horizon line, and then judge the distance on the wall from this point (V.P. No. 1) to the point of sight, by comparing this distance with that from the base of line X-Z to the P.S. A comparison of these measurements definitely fixes the vanishing point No. 1. In our diagram the distance from V.P. No. 1. to the P.S. is approximately one-and-a-half times that of the distance between X and P.S.

You now have to discover the *height* of the box, and this you can do by checking off, with your ruler at arm's length, the relative heights between X-Z and X-P.S. Next connect the top "Z" and base "X" to V.P. No. 1.

You have now the top and bottom edges, on one side of the box, drawn in perspective, and you should proceed in precisely the same manner to draw the side running to the V.P. No. 2, first discovering the approximate point where a rule continued along the line A cuts the horizon on the left—and fixing it by comparison of measurements, as you did in the case of V.P. No. 1. You can then connect X and Z to V.P. No. 2.

When you have done this, check, by your ruler, the apparent distance of the edge of the box B from the edge X-Z, and then draw another upright line. From where this edge B cuts the line C carry another line to V.P. No. 2, and you have the top of the further side of the box.

Proceed, in the same way, by comparative measurements to fix the positions of the edge D, connecting the top of this to the V.P. No. 1.

These general principles can be applied to all perspective problems and are an adequate *introduction* to the subject at this stage.

Now study Figure 66 of the church and gravestones. Here the churchyard wall is running straight away from us; therefore it vanishes to the point of sight. The long lines of the church, and the short sides of the nearest gravestone do so as well, while the end wall of the church and the long sides of the nearest gravestone are all parallel to us, therefore, they are drawn quite horizontal.

But notice the other four gravestones. They are placed at a *different angle*, and so they will vanish to two other points on the horizon line, the lines which run away from us toward the left, meeting at a vanishing point somewhere on the left, and the lines which run towards the right meeting at a vanishing point somewhere on the right.

These illustrations—though they deal with much more advanced problems than you will be expected to work out at present—are useful as illustrating one or two basic facts and principles of perspective.

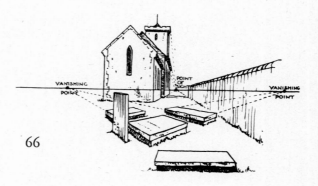

66

COMPOSITION

The accurate drawing of a group of objects, will not achieve an artistic result unless the arrangement, or pictorial composition is attractive.

Composition is not a mystery—nor is it a matter which can be left to chance, personal taste, or inspiration, unless you are an unusually gifted artist. It is a factor in Art which is based on certain rules and principles—though none of these is absolute.

For your convenience, therefore, several diagrams of forms of compositions in use from the past to the present time, are used to provide the illustrations of this lesson. The simplicity of these forms is very evident, and upon these few simple principles most of the best pictures have been based. These are the principal forms, and they are capable of unlimited varieties of application. It is, of course, quite likely that in time others will be added.

It will be noted that the majority of the diagrams illustrate composition of line, the remainder being examples of tone, or light and shade.

SOME CLASSICAL
AND MODERN
EXAMPLES

67. This is an example of light against dark repeated by dark against light, further interest being given by the form of line.

68. This is a rough note of the composition of one of the most dramatic of Rembrandt's pictures, the etching known as "The Three Trees." Here again the strongest dark is placed against the strongest light in the most dramatic manner possible.

69. This is a picture where the whole of the sky is in middle tone, and the interest is given and the effect of air and light intensified by the darks.

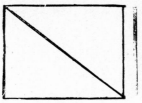 

Examples of composition by Cuyp, Turner, Raphael, Ostade, Corot and other masters.

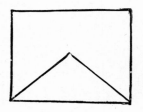 

70. The use of the angle in linear composition. The angle has been produced by a line drawn from the top-left-hand corner to the bottom right-hand corner, and the feeling given is, naturally, one of progression from top to bottom. If this feeling of progression were not stopped—by a black spot, for instance, as it has been in the sketch of a picture by Cuyp—the effect of this line would be one of continuing right out of the picture. The principal dark being placed against the light arrests the eye. It is this darkest dark, and the upright character of the mass, which balances the greater mass of half-tone at the left of the picture, and concentrates the pictorial interest. It can be understood that the picture would lack cohesion if the general details were allowed to struggle aimlessly out of the picture.

71. Turner. This is an equally simple form. It is circular and has lines radiating to a centre. This form of composition was greatly used by Turner. The reason for the two curved lines on the diagram is to show that the composition forms a segment only of a circle, as, if the whole circle were introduced the composition would be merely geometrical and inartistic.

72. Raphael. This is a conventional balanced composition. It is in the form of symmetrical scales, and although used greatly by the old religious painters, it is rarely employed, in the old way, by the moderns.

73. Ostade. This is the triangle or pyramid form of composition, and has been much used both by the ancients and the moderns, the feeling of stability given by the broad base being greatly liked. In this it will be noted that the complete triangle is not slavishly introduced, but the broad principle used. The student is advised to consider this form in composing groups.

74. This is the "slide-balance" form of com position. Anyone who has visited a railway station has probably seen a slide-balance, and knows that a very large weight placed near the axis can be balanced by a small weight at the farther end of the slide. A comparatively modern form of composition with landscape painters.

75. This is the L shape form of composition. It is one that was greatly used by Corot, and he achieved many beautiful effects by his use of it. It is more particularly adapted to landscape than to figure painting.

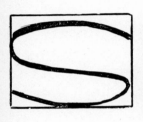 

76. The "S" and the zig-zag form of composition are nearly the same thing, and are used greatly by landscape painters with the idea of suggesting infinity of distance. The "S" form is also the most generally used with all figure painters, and the student can find countless examples in modern book and magazine illustration.

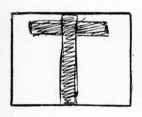 

77. The form of the cross is often used in composition both for figure and landscape pictures. It is liked by artists for the feeling of stability and dignity it imparts; in fact, if an artist can get into a composition, in an artistic way, many upright lines, he is sure to attain a feeling of dignity.

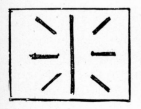 

78. This form of composition illustrates an "axial balance" on an upright, and is a form that was used in the olden times for scriptural pictures, especially those in which figures are depicted flying in the air. This is, of course simply another adaptation of Natures's principle of radiation to a centre, which I have already discussed.

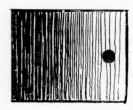

79. This diagram illustrates a form of balance in light and shade. If the student will place his finger on the black spot in this diagram, he will see that the general feeling is of a sense of progression from light to dark, namely from right to left, but immediately he removes his finger the black spot asserts its power, and, becoming the centre of attraction, balances the other movement.

80. This is an example of what is called strong contrast, and shows the darkest dark cutting against the lightest light in the sharpest manner possible, the lights and darks being afterwards united by gradation of halftones, thus giving great breadth of effect.

81. This is a natural form of angular composition showing a doorway, and in principle is exactly the same as the last, although in arrangement it definitely follows the examples in figure 70.

82. This form of composition shows what is known as an interchange. The first thing to be noted is that the picture is divided into two parts, light and middle tone. Then a spot of light is placed on the middle tone, and a spot of dark on the light. This is also a development of the angular composition, figure 70.

83. This form of composition is an example of silhouette treatment and explains itself.

You will notice, from these instances, that there are several forms of composition—all, in their way, justified. You will remember the first fact you were told—viz.: that there is *no absolute rule* regarding composition, but that everyone finds his own method of saying what he wants to say and how to say it. Why, then, have we given you these diagrams and details?

To show you what others have done before you, how they expressed themselves—how they "got out of the slough." They had to find their own way; you have to find yours; and in studying what others have done, you will be better able to avoid what is bad, and adapt what is good.

A MASTER
DRAUGHTSMAN

If you become as absorbed in the study of line drawing as most of my pupils are, you will not only develop your own technique enthusiastically, and study the methods of modern masters of line but will seek inspiration from the old masters. That search could easily prove a life-long delight to you, for there is a vast field for the pen-draughtsman to study, in the brilliant line technique of the old etchers, painters and draughtsmen.

You could spend months in a library, revelling in Holbein's drawings, in the superbly etched portraits by Van Dyck, in the etchings, sketches and studies by Rembrandt, in the magnificent draughtsmanship of Michelangelo, Leonardo, Rubens, Turner and Dürer, in the work of Salvator Rosa, Tiepolo and other masters.

Of the more modern men, Goya did two superb etchings of portraits by Velasquez, which are absolute models of light and shade for a pen-draughtsman to study; but as our space is severely limited, we can hardly do better than confine our present remarks to the line drawings of Albrecht Dürer, the painter, etcher, engraver and pen-draughtsman, who lived from 1471 to 1528.

ALBRECHT
DÜRER

There is a whole library of books on his life and work, but his drawings and studies can best be seen in the several volumes by Edler Von Schonbrunner and Dr. Freidrich Lippmann. In these books all his chief studies are reproduced exactly the same size as the originals; below, and on the following pages you will see some reproductions which will give you an idea of his varied technical methods.

Another comprehensive and fully illustrated record of his achievements is to be found in the three volumes by Freidrich Winkler, *Albrecht Dürer Zeichnungen*, published in Berlin in 1936.

Dürer has inspired most of the decorative book-illustrators since his time. The men of the 'sixties—Ford Madox Brown, Poynter, Millais, and other famous artists—were very obvious disciples of Dürer; while of the more modern men —Walter Crane, Linley Sambourne the *Punch* cartoonist, and Howard Pyle the American illustrator, are names which at once occur to one when thinking of Dürer's work. There are scores of others.

If ever you are in London, or near any big library which has a well-equipped Art section, ask to see the Dürer volumes. In the Print Room at the British Museum I have studied a large collection of his originals, as well as the books of reproductions mentioned above.

His wonderful pen study for the Crucifixion was drawn in sepia on buff paper, and though this reproduction, just about half the size of the original, hardly gives an adequate impression of the distinction of the original, the line quality is perfectly shown.

Observe the decision of the line throughout, the extraordinary simplicity and effectiveness with which the construction of the figure of Christ is suggested, and the completeness with which the light and shade is indicated.

The drapery is also specially worthy of note—as all Dürer's drapery invariably was. It is beautifully composed, arranged, and constructed, even in this comparatively hurried sketch.

As a contrast, turn to the drawing, in an utterly different manner, of the children's heads. Here he has worked in a loose, easy, realistic fashion, suggesting in the subtlest and most charming way the light and shade and the texture of his very difficult model. Only those who have tried to draw a baby's head in line can appreciate the mastery of these sketches which again, in the original, were drawn in sepia on a slightly tinted ground.

ALBRECHT DÜRER: PEN STUDY FOR THE "CRUCIFIXION"

The very remarkable studies on the next page were draw
in an entirely individual way. They were about three time
the size of these reproductions, and the lighter line-shadin
which you will see, was not, as you might imagine, pen worl
but white lines put in with the point of a brush. The darke
tones were introduced with lamp black, used—not as in th
customary water-colour method—but in *lines*. The studies
therefore, may be described as line drawings with the brusl

The surface on which Dürer worked was a prepared boar
originally of white, but obviously flat-tinted with blue, grey
or greenish tone, slightly mixed with white to form a chalk
like ground.

The beauty of these drawings is so obvious that they hard
ly call for detailed criticism, but, you will find it very difficu
to discover, as a study, anything more appealing, on accour
of its absolute sincerity and reverence, than the prayin,
hands; while, in the drapery, the subtle observation of the ligh
and shade is as remarkable as the wonderful way in which h
has drawn the folds.

*   *   *

CONCLUSION

In these pages, I have only been able to introduce you to
few aspects of the vast and inexhaustible field of Art whicl
has been the absorbing enthusiasm of my life and whicl
may, I trust, provide you with infinite pleasure. It was witl
that hope that I embarked on this book.

If, in the past, you wished you could draw, I believe tha
your wish is now far nearer to fulfilment. But to achieve
your ambition you must bring your own enthusiasm to the
work. Nature does not achieve her miracles carelessly; the
are the result of a carefully-planned, logical sequence o
growth. So it must be with you, if you want to draw by
Nature's methods.

If, during your study of this book you have found your
self in need of further guidance, do not hesitate to write tc
me about your problems. For it will be a privilege to share
with you some of the delights which Art has brought to me

I have touched, in this book, upon many differen
branches of drawing from Nature and life, I have discussed

STUDIES IN LIGHT
AND SHADE

the drawing of animals and architecture, outlined the principles of perspective and composition, and reminded you of the inspiration you can obtain from the work of the Old Masters.

The study of painting, and a detailed consideration of the methods of drawing used by famous artists of the past and present, will be the subjects of later volumes. Meanwhile, it may be that one special branch of art has already set alight your enthusiasm, and your wish to concentrate on that aspect of drawing.

Whatever may be the corner of the field which you desire to study, I shall be most willing to advise you, and help you to develop your work on the soundest of all foundations— those of Nature herself.

P.V.B.